AF540832

Underachievement in Biology

By

Dr. H.V. Vamadevappa

Department of Post-graduate Studies and Research in Education
B.E.A. College of Education
Davangere–577004
Karnataka

DISCOVERY PUBLISHING HOUSE
NEW DELHI

First Published-2006

ISBN 81-8356-085-7

Published by

DISCOVERY PUBLISHING HOUSE

4831/24, Ansari Road, Prahlad Street,
Darya Ganj, New Delhi-110002 (India)
Phone: 23279245 • Fax: 91-11-23253475
E-mail:dphtemp@indiatimes.com

Printed at
Arora Offset Press
Laxmi Nagar, Delhi–92

DEDICATED

TO

MY BELOVED PARENTS

Who are the Prime Movers in my Life

Preface

Wholesome development of the child is the primary concern of any established educational system. The academic development of the individual is the most important component of wholesome development. There are differences in the attainment of academic skills among individuals moreover academic development is seldom homogeneous in the same individual. Further the most important issue in the academic development is often not in consonance with his ability and this brings us to the problem of underachievement which has been baffling researchers for several decades. Hence, underachievement signifies that the student has not made the most of his abilities. It denotes that despite high potentialities, the student is lagging behind in academic achievement.

While discussing the achievement of the student, the Education Commission (1964-66) observes that the problem of academic underachievement is of great concern to a developing country like India. Extraordinary talent unidentified, undeveloped and unexplored is a tremendous waste. The commission has also mentioned the need for diagnosing the causes of low achievement, which hinders the underachievers in coming up to the level of their full potential abilities and then to provide remedial treatment.

To a developing country like India, this challenge is of great social significance as it involves colossal wastage of human potential and resources. Therefore, it has to be encountered with profound care lest it shake the very roots of nation's economic and social structure. Also one of the challenges before educationists is to help each individual to achieve his optimum. Thus the author explored scientifically the causal factors relating to underachievement in Biology among pre-university students.

In this book the author has discussed various aspects of different psychological and social factors and their relationships with academic achievement in order to highlight the dimension of the problem of underachievement in Biology among Pre-university students. He has substantiated his discussions by empirical data collected on a sample of Biology Students selected from 10 Pre-university Colleges of Chitradurga District in Karnataka State.

This study has lead to the identification of causes of underachievement in Biology among Pre-university students. The author has offered some valuable suggestions or recommendations for taking remedial measures on the basis of research findings.

I owe my deepest gratitude to my esteemed guide Dr. M.M. Pattanashetti, Professor & Research Guide, M.M. College of Education, Davangere and Dr. D.S. Shivananda, Professor (Rtd.), Bangalore University, Bangalore for their able guidance and constant encouragement.

I am grateful to Discovery Publishing House, New Delhi for taking keen interest to make the book the best.

This book will be of great use to teachers and students of Education and all those concerned with planning policy making and Development of Education in India.

Dr. H.V. Vamadevappa

Acknowledgement

The author expresses his sincere and deep gratitude to Dr. P. Basavakumaraiah. Ph.D., Dean. Faculty of Education and Chairman of Post-graduate Studies in Education, Kuvempu University for giving his valuable suggestions, professional motivation, constant encouragement and concern.

The author takes this opportunity to record his most sincere and heartfelt gratitude to his esteemed guide, Dr. M.M. Pattanashetti, Ph.D., Professor in Education. M.M. College of Education and Visiting Professor, Post-graduate Department of Education, B.E.A., College of Education, Davangere, for his valuable guidance, inspiring suggestions and the keen interest evinced by him in the successful completion of this research work.

The author expresses his indelible indebtedness and deep sense of gratitude to Dr. D.S. Shivananda, Ph.D., Principal. Sarvagna College of Education, Bangalore, whose constant inspiration and valuable suggestions at every stage of this research have enabled me to complete this investigation.

The author is highly grateful to Dr. G.M. Patted. Professor of Education (Retd.). P.G. Department of Education, Karnataka University, Dharwad for giving his valuable suggestions in finalizing the format of this study.

The author expresses his sincere thanks to Dr. H.V. Shivashankara, Ph.D., Professor and Research Guide in Department of Post-graduate Studies and Research in

Education and Principal, M.M. College of Education, Davangere for his timely encouragement and support given to me in conducting research.

The author is grateful to Dr. B.S. Nagi, Senior Research Fellow, Council for Social Development, New Delhi and Prof. Sangam, J.J.M. Medical College, Davangere for the help rendered by them in analyzing the data and in providing computer facilities for the analysis.

The author's heartfelt thanks are due to Sri. Y.M. Vittal Rao, Professor, M.M. College of Education, Davangere and my other colleagues, for their enthusiastic and whole hearted co-operation in successful completion of this work.

The author is also grateful to the members of the Faculty of Post-graduate Department of Education, B.E.A. College of Education, Davangere for their co-operation while conducting this study.

The author is thankful to all the Heads, Biology Lecturers and first year P.U.C. Science students of selected Pre-University Colleges of Chitradurga District for their whole hearted support and co-operation during the collection of data for the study.

The author express his sincere thanks to Kuvempu University and Sri. Taralabalu Jagadguru Education Society, Sirigere for having permitted me to conduct this study.

The author is thankful to Sri. K.S. Veerabhadraiah, Lecturer in English, Government P.U. College, Channagiri, for his valuable assistance in the preparation of this book and he also thanks Sri Dayanand, Librarian, B.E.A., College of Education for having extended his help in providing of library facilities.

The author's heartfelt thanks are due to his wife Smt. G.M. Sudha, whose painstaking efforts in scoring of the answer scripts with me have enabled to complete the work well in time.

I thank Mr. Iqbal Hussain. M/s. CTDC, Vidyanagar, for precise typing and laser printing.

Finally, I thank all my well-wishers, family members and friends for their constant concern, encouragement and constructive criticisms.

H.V. Vamadevappa

Contents

1

Introduction

Background of the Study

Academic achievement has always been the centre of educational research and despite many varied statements about the aims of education, the academic development of a child continues to be the primary and the most important goal of education. Not that other aspects of educational objectives are ignored, but the fact remains that academic achievement is the unique responsibility of all educational institutions established by the society to promote a wholesome scholastic development of a child.

As individual differences in academic achievement were observed at each level in each grade, researchers interested themselves in studying these, especially the conditions responsible for the differential achievement products. Amongst the many factors which influenced academic achievement, it was seen that intelligence contributed substantially to the variations in the academic achievement scores. The relationship between intelligence and achievement is by no means perfect and suggests the role of some non-intellectual factors in the scholastic development of a child. The interest has now shifted to studying conditions which lead to low achievement in spite of the high intellectual level. Accordingly in the past three decades some studies were devoted to underachievement.

Since the present study is concerned with the identification of some factors causing underachievement in

Biology among the pre-university students, it is pertinent to consider at this stage the concept of underachievement, in order to understand the psychological and educational effects. The present chapter is intended to analyse the concept of underachievement and to display the theoretical view of the same. The concept of underachievement is a vital problem in modern education. The amount of the incidence of underachievement in an educational system is interpreted broadly as a measure of its inefficiency. Therefore, it is important to find out the factors causing underachievement to give special attention to underachievers.

Genesis of the Problem

The Pre-university examination results indicate that Biology is one of the subjects in which considerable number of students fail each year. There may be various reasons for this. The public and the parents find fault with the teachers and the education system as a whole. The teachers attribute the failure to the poor conditions of the school, the lack of interest and low socio-economic status of the learners. The factors affecting the achievement of pupils may be classified as psychological, sociological and academic. The interaction of these factors influence the achievement of the pupils.

The results of various pre-university colleges in Chitradurga District clearly state that many students who are sufficiently intelligent and score high marks in other science subjects, do not get comparable marks in Biology. This is a problem requiring close scrutiny. To look into this problem, the investigator interviewed some second year Pre-University students who have secured less marks in first year Pre-University Biology when compared to other science subjects. Researcher also administered a questionnaire to know their problems and causes for the low achievement in Biology. Based on responses of the pupils, the investigator selected some factors that are considered to be causal factors related to underachievement in Biology among Pre-University students.

District wise result of second year Pre-University science students was collected from Karnataka state Pre-University board. It clearly show that Chitradurga, Bangalore rural, Raichur, Mandya and Kolar districts performed very poorly during the last six years. Out of these, Chitradurga district with an average percentage of 29.78 is selected randomly for the present study.[14]

Need and Importance of the Study

The high ability student whose scholastic performance is low is usually referred to in education literature as the underachiever. (24:5614-A) Research evidence indicates that the underachiever has been the subject of continuing concern of parent sand educators at all levels. The studies (Stoner 1956), Miller 1965, Srivastava 1967, Pal and Sexena 1970, Sexena 1972, Menon 1973, Agarwal 1976, Ghuman 1976, Tandon 1977, Sharma 1978 and Puri 1987) that have dealt with the underachiever reveals various and differing foci and thus suggest a multifaceted nature of the problem of the underachievers.

While discussing the achievement of the students the Education Commission (1964-66) observes that the problem of academic underachievement is of great concern to a developing country. Extraordinary talent unidentified, undeveloped and unexplored is a tremendous waste. The Commission has also mentioned the need for diagnosing the causes of low achievement which hinders the underachievers in coming up to the level of their full potential abilities and then to provide remedial treatment (13:428).

Underachievement is a grave problem from the economic and social points of view because it involves wastage of human and economic resources and it is a problem from the learner's point of view also as it causes emotional unrest and psychological tension. It causes problems not only to the underachieving students, but also to their parents and teachers. Since the cause of underachievement lies with the society for not having provided adequate opportunities to develop one's potential, it has a social obligation towards underachievers.

Underachievement, as a psychological concept, refers to a loss of potential man-power. Any society cannot remain indifferent to this problem if it is concerned with its human resources. However, not many investigations into the important problem have been made. Of these, a few studies (Srivastava 1967, Pal and Saxena 1970, Saxena 1972, Menon 1973, Agarwal 1976, Ghuman 1976, Tandon 1977, Sharma 1978 and Puri 1987) related to academic underachievement and the factors significantly associated with this phenomenon are available.

Wholesome or maximum development of the child is the primary concern of any established educational system. The academic development of the individual is the most important component of wholesome development. There are differences in the attainment of learning (academic) skills among individuals, moreover academic development is seldom homogeneous in the same individual. Further the most important issue in the academic development is often not in consonance with his ability and this brings us to the problem of underachievement which has been baffling researchers for several decades. Hence underachievement signifies that the student has not made the most of his abilities. It denotes that despite high potentialities, the student is lagging behind in academic achievement. This indeed is a great challenge which has to be met with great care because it involves serious loss to the individual leading to self undervaluation, reflections of which are seen in unhappiness, frustration, revolt and withdrawal.

To a developing country like ours, this challenge is of great social significance as it involves colossal wastage of human potential. Therefore, it has to be encountered with profound care lest it should shake the very roots of nation's economic and social structure. Also one of the cardinal problems before educationist's is to help each individual to achieve his optimum. Thus, the need for exploring scientifically the causal factors relating to underachievement is imperative.

When a student's academic performance falls short of the level commensurate with this mental abilities, he is said to be an underachiever. As the investigator is interested in finding the causes of underachievement in Biology, it is worth to quote the words of Education Commission (1964-66) about the importance of teaching Biology. In the words of Education Commission. The concept of Biology as a method of inquiry by means of accurate and confirmable observations, quantitatively and mathematically analysed and controlled experimentation should be impressed on the minds of young learners (13:345)

The National Policy on Education—1986 has laid greater emphasis on the teaching of science and has made following recommendations; science education will be strengthened so as to develop in the child well defined abilities and values such as the spirit of inquiry, creativity, objectivity, the courage to question and an aesthetic sensibility. Science education programmes will be designed to enable the learner to acquire problem solving and decision making skills and to discover the relationship of science with health agriculture industry and other aspects of daily life. (28:149)

Biology is one of the core subjects taught at the pre-university science classes. It occupies an important place in the pre-university science curriculum because of its utilitarian, disciplinary, aesthetic and cultural values. It is a matter of common experience of lecturers teaching Biology that although many students have the capacity to learn well, their actual performance in Biology examinations is poor.

Many of studies in India and abroad have concentrated research mainly at the secondary level. The investigator feels that the pre-university course is an important stage in the education of an individual. It is a stage to select diversified courses in his educational career. Most of the pre-university science students are aspiring for professional/technical/higher courses. In order to fulfil their desire, they will put maximum efforts in the academic work. In spite of this many students will achieve less than their potential ability. In addition to this, Karnataka State Pre-University Board introduced a new syllabus for the pre-university classes from the academic year 1995-96. The investigator decided to find out the causes of underachievement in Biology among the pre-university students, since the studies in this specific area are conscious by their absence.

Statement of the Problem

The problem of the present investigation is—"*An Investigation into the Factors Causing Underachievement in Biology among the First Year Pre-University Students of Chitradurga District*".

Objectives of the Study

The present study was undertaken with the following broad objectives:

(i) To identify the underachievers in Biology among the first year pre-university students.

(ii) To identify the causes of underachievement in Biology among the first year pre-university students.

(iii) To suggest measures for the improvement of achievement of underachievers in Biology in the light of the identified causes of underachievement.

Specific Objectives of the Study

(a) To find out whether low attitude towards science is the cause of underachievement in Biology among the first year pre-university students.

(b) To find out whether low achievement motivation is the cause of the underachievement in Biology among the first year pre-university students.

(*c*) To find out whether poor study habits is the cause of underachievement in Biology among the first year pre-university students.

(*d*) To find out whether poor adjustment is the cause of underachievement in Biology among the first year pre-university students.

(*e*) To find out whether higher comprehensive anxiety is the cause of underachievement in Biology among the first year pre-university students.

(*f*) To find out whether low self-concept is the cause of underachievement in Biology among the first year pre-university students.

(*g*) To find out whether low socio-economic status is the cause of underachievement in Biology among the first year pre-university students.

The Concept of Underachievement

High and low achievements refer only to above and below average achievers, the concept of over and underachievement takes into account the academic achievement in relation to the intellectual level of the individual (6:6) Especially with respect to intelligence, wide variations have been observed amongst different individuals. Without going into the detailed discussion about the relative influences of heredity and environment upon the intellectual development of a student, a very rational and logical position on this problem as mentioned by Skinner suggests that though the intellectual capacity of the individual can be increased by educational and other environmental factors, the highest limit to be reached by that individual is already set by hereditary factors which are beyond human control. Education at best helps each individual to reach the maximum of his abilities. If we accept this position, we shall not expect every student to achieve at the same level and some of the low achievers cannot probably be blamed for low achievement, because they might really be doing their best on the basis of what nature has endowed them with. The question, therefore, shifts to those who achieve low not because they lack the ability but on account of certain other forces, that is their achievement is low in spite of their higher abilities and potentialities for better achievement. It is their group of underachievers which poses a great challenge to educators because they possess the intellectual equipment but still are lagging behind others in achievement. It should be pointed out that overachievers are defined as those who achieve higher than what is expected to their intellectual level. (6:6) Unfortunately, in India not much research work has been undertaken in this field.

Lewis (1941) called those children underachievers whose educational ages are one year or more, lower than their mental ages. (21:2-3)

Holmes and Finley (1957) described underachievement in terms of grade placement deviation (GPD) as GPD = AGP-CAGP + K

Where AGP = Actual grade placement

CAGP = Grade placement expected from chronological age

GPD = Grade placement deviation

K = Constant of 0.5 intended to give all values a positive sign (18:3)

Goldberg (1959) identified those as underachievers whose IQ is above 120 but grades (achievement) are below 80 per cent of the class standing. (12:3)

Dowd (1962) called those students as underachievers who exceed 90 per cent of their classmates for scholastic aptitude but fail to exceed 50 per cent academically. (8:3)

Hildereth (1966) called those as underachievers who stand in the upper third or quarter of their class in ability as measured by objective tests, but fail in the middle or lower segment in achievement either in a particular subject or in his school work as a whole. (17:3)

Gallagher (1979) defined underachieving gifted students as those who exhibit as gap between achievement test scores and intelligence test scores. (10:4)

After going through the definitions of various researchers, the researcher conceptually defines underachievement as. The achievement of the student which is not commensurate with his potentialities.

Incidence of Underachievement

The phenomenon of underachievement is not seen to be alike in all cases. There is variation from one sample to another, depending upon several factors associated with the sample studied. It is likely to depend upon the efficiency of the school system and to every large extent, on the effectiveness of the teacher. The factors which cause underachievement in some subjects need not necessarily cause underachievement in other subjects. Researchers have not yet found out as to what extent underachievement occurs. Accurate data concerning the incidence of underachievement are not generally available.

Some studies point out that a certain percentage of underachievement is not unnatural. Bricklin & Bricklin suggest that 15 per cent to 40 per cent of all school children fall under the category of underachievers.[4] In another study, Dhaliwal and Saini reported 44.91, 47.46, 48.31 and 50.85 per cent of pupils are underachieving in English, Maths, Geography and Hindi respectively.(7:90) According to Gowan, a ten per cent underachievement is a common feature of gifted students. (15:117-119)

Tolor has conducted a study on the incidence of underachievement. His sample consisted of 1263 High school students of a suburban community. He computed the correlation coefficient between OTIS and National Educational

Development Test (NEDP), using regression equations, the subjects were classified into overachievers; normal achievers and underachievers. The incidence of underachievement was found to be around 26 per cent with the NEDP composite score as achievement criterion. (32:63-65)

Some studies conducted in Kerala gave a rough indication of students who under achieve in different subjects. In a study of underachievement in English in secondary school students of Kerala by Abraham, it was seen that about 15 per cent of the students were underachievers. (1:340) Similarly, Mathew found that about 16 per cent of the secondary students were underachievers in Science. (23:77-80) For Secondary School Mathematics, it was noticed by Nair that nearly 28 per cent of High Intelligence Group are underachievers. [26] Beedawat Sher Singh reports that the incidence of underachievement is significantly higher in the schools and underachievement in the science group is the biggest of all the groups. (3:188). Iyer reported about 14 per cent of the High Intelligence Group are underachievers. (19:668) Nagpal. R. Reported that 10 per cent of Engineering students were underachievers at Indian Institute of Technology, New Delhi, (25:677-678) Sankaran Nair reported about 16 per cent of the high school students were underachievers in Biology.[27] Shahpur reported about 38-40 per cent of Secondary school students were underachievers in Mathematics. (29:83)

Thus, there is no uniformity in the studies regarding the incidence of underachievement. It has been pointed out that Intelligence Quotient, when it is a pure measure of intelligence, accounts for 25 per cent of the variance in attainment (5:280-296). So that even if there were no individual differences in intelligence, the individual difference in performance would still be 75 per cent of what they now are. Havighurst et al. have suggested that nearly 50 per cent of the best human material is not developed any where near capacity.[16]

Persistance of Underachievement

Investigators like Spiering[31] and Barret (2:192-194) hold that underachievement is an enduring phenomenon and as such underachievers must be subjected to a study from time to time.

Goldman is of the view that those leaving schools would perform better when they enter colleges and this view is shared by other authorities also.[11] As a contradiction to this Shaw and Mc Cuen have concluded that underachievement can be identified in the early elementary school years and with the increase of age, underachievement also increases. (30:103-108) Frankel's findings also support that the incidence of underachievement persists throughout senior high school. (9:172-180)

Similar study of Wageman confirm the above views, the study was about the persistence of the incidence of overachievement, normal achievement and underachievement at the University of Illinois for one Semester. He came to the conclusion that overachievers, normal achievers and underachievers of high school tended to remain as such at the university also. (33:383-389)

Kowitz and Armstrong have studied the persistence of underachievement. Their study on 259 boys and 231 girls from elementary school to junior high school level showed that underachievement is a common phenomenon among school children and is persisting at all levels of education. (20:207-211)

Education and Underachievement

Low achievement as well as underachievement is a crucial problem that needs urgent solution so as to enable the society to derive optimum benefits from the system of education. While low achievement needs special treatment by educators, teachers and others involved in the system, underachievement can be reduced to a minimum, if not eliminated completely, by identifying the contributing factors and reducing them to the minimum. Before the factors are subjected to investigation, underachievement itself has to be identified. Though it is necessary to identify underachievement at different stages during the course of a student's educational career, there is a strong view that it is unfair to label a youngster an underachiever, for once he is labelled, he is labelled forever and very often the label is erroneous in many respects.

According to Wellington and Wellington, the guess that a child is an underachiever is not enough, because guesses even by professionals have been proved to be incorrect by researchers. Wellington and Wellington point out on the basis of their experience with underachievers, that these students are not happy to be treated as underachievers. In their opinion those with higher, potential are despondent when their achievement is low and hence they should be helped to work upto their capacity. The modern school has no desire to neglect a child who does not achieve his best, though this best may vary from person to person. Therefore, earnest attempts have been made for detecting the reasons for failure and low achievements and distinguish those performances from underachievement. (34:1)

The incidence of low achievement is due to deficient intellectual ability but underachievement implies the system's failure to utilize the potential in full. The Education Commission (1964-66) has rightly made it clear that the failure of underachievers should be of special concern to the developing nations who cannot lose this potential man-power especially within the higher capacity range.(13:428) The larger interest of the country enjoins us to adopt suitable teaching-learning strategies to prevent underachievement and to make suitable adjustments to the individual learner's capacities, needs and interests. Thus, it becomes an essential part of the educational system to devise methods of identification and treatment of underachievement so as to develop the system of education that stands for the all round development of the individual.

Scope of the Problem

The present study has tried to study the problem of underachievement in Biology among first year pre-university students of Chitradurga district. The investigator has tried to identify the underachievers and studied the relationship of the following factors namely. Attitude towards Science, Achievement motivation, Study habits, Adjustment, Comprehensive Anxiety, Self-concept and Socio-economic status with overachievers, normal achievers and underachievers in Biology. Sample covers the randomly selected rural and urban pre-university colleges' first year pre-university science students of Chitradurga district.

Resume of the Succeeding Chapters

The research report is presented in five chapters. The chapter plan is as follows Chapter 1 titled introduction, which deals with the background of the study which consists of genesis of the problem, need and importance of the study, statement of the problem and objectives of the study. It has also dealt with the concept of underachievement, incidence of underachievement, persistence of underachievement, education and underachievement, and scope of the problem.

Chapter 2 titled review of related literature, deals with the review of related studies which helped the researcher to design the present study. First section deals with the reviews related to factors causing academic underachievement among eleventh standard/intermediate/higher secondary students. The second section deals with the reviews related to causes of underachievement in Biology.

Chapter 3 under the heading Methodology of the study, gives the details regarding selection of variables, discussion and definitions of variables and terms, identification of over, normal and underachievers, hypotheses needed to be tested, description of the various tools used for the collection of data, sampling, administration and scoring of the test, and statistical techniques used for analysis of data.

Chapter 4 titled analysis and interpretation of data deals with analysis techniques, tables, figures and description of findings pertinent to each hypothesis. In this chapter, the research hypotheses set-up have been tested by using single classification ANOVA and comparison of means using DUNCAN'S procedure.

Chapter 5 titled summary of the findings and suggestions, deals with the brief summary of the earlier chapters, findings and conclusions of the study, educational implications of the study, limitations of the study and suggestions for further research.

REFERENCES

1. Abraham, M, "Some Factors Relating to Underachievement in English of Secondary School Pupils". In Buch,.M.B. (Ed.), *Second Survey of Research in Education,* Baroda: Society for Education Research and Development, 1979.
2. Barret, H.G. "An Intensive Study of 32 Gifted Children". *Personnel and Guidance Journal,* 36, 1957, pp. 192-194.
3. Beedawat, Sher Singh. "A Study of Academic Underachievement Among Students". University of Rajasthan, 1976, *Indian Dissertation Abstracts,* 12, 14, Jan.-Dec. 1984, p. 188.
4. Bricklin, P. and Bricklin, P.M. *Bright Poor Grades: The Psychology of Underachievement.* New York: Delacorte Press. 1966.
5. Cattel, R.B., Sealey, A.P. and Sevency, A.B. "What can Personality and Motivation Service Traits Measurement Add to the Prediction of School Achievement?" *British Journal of Educational Psychology,* 36, 1966, pp. 280-296.
6. Deo, Prathibha. "Underachievers: A Challenge to Educators". *NIE Journal,* 2, 4, March 1968, p. 6.
7. Dhaliwal, A.S. and Saini, B.S. "A Study of the Prevalence of Academic Underachievement Among High School Students". *Educational Review,* 10, 1, Jan. 1975, pp. 90-107.
8. Dowd, R.J. "Underachieving Students of High Capacity". J. Higher Education, 22, 1962, 327-330. In Maitra, Krishna. Gifted Underachievers—A Challenge in Education. New Delhi: Discovery Publishing House, 1991, p. 3.

9. Frankel, E. "A Comparative Study of Achieving and Underachieving High School Boys of High Intellectual Ability". *Journal of Educational Research,* 53, Jan. 1960, pp. 172-180.

10. Gallagher, J.J. Teaching of the Gifted Child, Allyn and Bacon, Inc., Boston, 1979. In Maitra, Krishna. *Gifted Underachievers—A Challenge in Education.* New Delhi: Discovery Publishing House, 1991, p. 4.

11. Goldaman, L. *Using Test in Counselling,* New York: Appleton—century Crofts, 1961.

12. Goldberg, M.L. "A 3 year Exceptional Progress at Dwitt Clinton High School to help bright Underachievers". High Points, 41, 1959, 5-35. In Maitra, Krishna. *Gifted Underachievers—A Challenge in Education.* New Delhi: Discovery Publishing House, 1991. p. 3.

13. Government of India. *Report of the Education Commission (1964-66).* Education and National Development, New Delhi: Ministry of Education, 1966.

14. Government of Karnataka. *Statistics of the Second Year Pre-University Result (1992-1996).* Bangalore: Karnataka State Pre-University Board, 1996.

15. Gowan, J.C. "Underachievement Revisited". *High School Journal,* 48, 1964, pp. 117-119.

16. Havighurst, R.J. Stevena, E. and Dehaan, H.F. "A Survey of Education of the Gifted Children". Chicago: *Supplementary Educational Monograph,* No. 33, Univ. of Chicago Press, 1955.

17. Hildreth, G.H. Introduction to the Gifted. Mc Graw Hill Books Inc. New York, 1966. In Maitra, Krishna. *Gifted Underachievers—A Challenge in Education,* New Delhi: Discovery Publishing House, 1991, p. 3.

18. Holmes, J.A. and Finley, C.G. "Underage and Overage Grade Placements and School Achievement". J. Edu. Psychol, 48, 1957, 447-547. In Maitra, Krishna. *Gifted Underachievers—A Challenge in Education,* New Delhi: Discovery Publishing House, 1991, p. 3.

19. Iyer. K.K. "Some Factors Related to Underachievement in Mathematics of Secondary School Students". 1977. In Buch, M.B. (Ed.), *Third Survey of Research in Education,* New Delhi: N.C.E.R.T., 1987.

20. Kowitz, G.T. and Armstrong, C.M. "Patterns of Academic Development". *Journal of Educational Development,* 2, 1965, pp. 207-211.

21. Lewis, N.D.C. A Short History of Psychiatric Achievement. New York: Basic Book, 1941, In Maitra, Krishna. *Gifted Underachievers—A Challenge in Education.* New Delhi: Discovery Publishing House, 1991, pp. 2-3.

22. Maitra. K. *Gifted Underachievers: A Challenge in Education.* New Delhi: Discovery Publishing House, 1991.

23. Mathew, Thomas. "Some Personality Factors Related to Underachievement in Science". University of Kerala, 1976. *Indian Dissertation Abstract,* Jan. –March 1979, pp. 77-80.

24. Matsunaga, Allen Sadao. "A Comparative Study of Ninth Grade Male Underachievers and Achievers on Selected Factors related to Achievement". 1971. *Dissertation Abstracts International,* 32, 10, April 1972, p. 5614-A.

25. Nagpal, R. "A Study of Non Intellectual Characteristics of Over and Underachieving Engineering Students". In Buch, M.B. (Ed.), *Third Survey of Research in Education,* New Delhi: N.C.E.R.T., 1987.

26. Nair, Jagannadan, *Identification of Some Personality Variables which Discriminate between High Intelligence Normal Achievers and High Intelligence Underachievers in Maths.* Unpublished M.Ed., Dissertation, University of Kerala, 1974.

27. Nair, Sankaran C.K. *"Factors Related to Underachievement in Biology of Secondary School Students".* Unpublished Doctoral Dissertation, University of Calicut, 1987.

28. National Council of Education Research and Training. *National Policy on Education-1986.* Resource Material. New Delhi: N.C.E.R.T., 1987.

29. Shahapur, N.P. *An Investigation into the Causes of Underachievement in Secondary School Mathematics".* Unpublished Doctoral Dissertation, Karnataka University, Dharwad, 1994.

30. Shaw, M.C. and Mc. Cuen. "The Aspect of Academic Underachievement of Bright Children". *Journal of Educational Psychology,* 51, 1960, pp. 103-108.

31. Spiering, M.F. *A Study of Past Achievement Patterns of Achievement and Underachieving Eighth Grade Students.* Published Doctoral Dissertation, University of Fordham, 1963.

32. Tolor, Alexander. "Incidence of Underachievement at the High School Level". *The Journal of Educational Research,* 63, 2, Oct. 1969, pp. 63-65.

33. Wageman. "Persistence of Ability—Achievement Discrepancies and Kuder Scores". *Personnel and Guidance Journal,* 43, 1964, pp. 383-389.

34. Wellington, C.B., and Wellington, J. *The Underachievers: Challenges and Guidelines.* Chicago: Rand Mc. Nally Curriculum Series, Rand Mc Nally and Company, 1964.

2

Review of Related Literature

In the previous chapter the background of the study in terms of genesis of the problem, need and importance of the study, statement of the problem, objectives of the study, the concept of underachievement, persistence of underachievement, education and underachievement and the scope of the problem are presented. In this chapter a brief review of studies related to factors causing academic underachievement are in the first section and the reviews related to causes of underachievement in Biology are presented in the second section.

The review of related literature is an important part of the scientific approach and is carried out in all areas of scientific research. This provides the research the means of getting to the frontier in his particular field of knowledge. It helps to understand the theory in the field and gives knowledge with regard to the procedures and instruments which have proved useful. It avoids unintentional replication of previous studies and keeps the researcher in a better position to interpret the significance of his own results. Thus, it could be seen that the review of related literature is a very important and essential step in designing any research work.

In this chapter, review of studies conducted in this area are discussed and presented.

Review Related to Factors Causing Academic Underachievement

Many studies were carried out to find out the various factors leading to underachievement both in India and abroad. The vast amount of material related to academic under achievement helped the research in getting a broad perspective of the various factors, which were resulting in the form of underachievement. A brief description of the studies conducted only on XI Standard/Intermediate College/Higher secondary students are discussed in the following section.

Marion Elizabeth Armstrong (1955) attempted to discover why some higher secondary students with average and above average ability fail to work to capacity while others of like ability are achieving normally, a study was conducted on the interests and social adjustment of underachievers as they compared to a matched group of normal achievers.

Five hypotheses were proposed as follows:

Underachievers are more likely than normal achievers. (1) To have stated vocational goals which are not in line with their dominant interests. (2) to be following vocational goals set for them by others or to have no vocational goals, (3) to have interests which are not satisfied by the school such as out door activity involving much moving about and action, but activities which require little continuous concentration. (4) not to be chosen for positions of responsibility and to show preference for relationships which are free from conflict, (5) to seek companions older or younger than themselves and to feel that they do not belong to groups of their own age.

Sample has been drawn from grades 9 and 11. The tools used were—the Otis quick scoring mental ability test. Gamma form, Kuder preference records vocational and personal. Rating scales on "co-operation", "dependability" and "judgement". Otis IQ scores and the average of school marks were correlated, underachievers were identified with the help of prediction equation. Chi-square was used as a test of significance for all comparisons between underachievers and normal achievers.

The findings of the study were as follows:

Underachievers were found more often (1) to have chosen their future occupations because of the influence of others. (2) to have future vocational goals which did not agree with their dominant interests as measured by the Kuder preference record-vocational, (3) to have obtained a greater number of low scores on the computational scale f the Kuder preference-vocational, (4) to have obtained more low scores in the area of "Preference for avoiding conflict" as measured by the Kuder preference record—personal, (5) to have obtained lower ratings on co-operation, dependability and judgement, (6) to prefer companions older than themselves (boys only), (7) to have obtained a smaller number of high scores on the computational scale of the Kuder preference record—vocational, (8) not to have been chosen for positions of responsibility in extra curricular activities (girls only).

Hypotheses confirmed were as follows:

Underachievers were more likely than normal achievers. (1) to be following vocational goals set for them by others. (2) to have stated goals not in line with their dominant interests. (3) to prefer outdoor activity, (4) to have been chosen less often for positions of responsibility (girls only) (5) to prefer companions older than themselves (boys only).

Hypotheses unconfirmed were as follows:

Underachievers were more likely than normal achievers (1) to have no stated vocational goals, (2) to prefer activity requiring much moving about but little concentration, (3) to feel that they did not belong to their own age group, (4) to prefer relationships which were free from conflict. (2:1349-1350)

William Gerald Stoner (1956) undertook an exploratory study of factors, other than intelligence, which were related to the underachievement of high ability students. The subjects were 1160 eleventh grade students of California. From this group 275 students with IQs of 120 or higher, as measured by Mc Nemar Test of mental ability, were selected for this study. The IOWA High school content examination was administered to the 275 students. An underachievers group was selected to include the 35 students who were lowest in the percentile score on the total test. An achiever group was selected to include 35 students who were highest in percentile score.

Treatment of the data indicated a significant difference (5 per cent level) between the means of the underachievers and achievers in total achievement test score and IQ score. To control the variable of intelligence, underachievers were matched with achievers on the basis of IQ score. This procedure yielded a matched group of 19 pairs of students. The difference between the mean IQ score for the matched group was not significant. The difference between the mean achievement test score for the matched group remained significant.

The diagnostic reading tests survey section was administered to the members of the matched group. Treatment of the data indicated a significant difference (5 per cent level) between the underachievers and the achievers in the area of comprehension and total test score.

The California psychological inventory was administered to the matched group. Treatment of the data indicated significant differences (5 per cent level) between underachievers and achievers on five of the seventeen scales which were scored.

A wide range of data from the unmatched group of 35 underachievers and 35 achievers was collected. A questionnaire of 180 items was developed to provide descriptive information about the group.

General conclusions drawn from the above study were:

1. The results from the reading tests indicate that the underachievers have more reading handicaps than the

achievers and comprehend less well the type of reading material measured by this test.

2. The underachievers are described by the following adjectives associated with the 5 scales of the California Psychological Inventory:

   (a) Dominance—common place; indifferent inhibited; retiring; silent; unassuming.

   (b) Socialization—defensive; demanding; opinionated; resentful; stubborn.

   (c) Intellectual efficiency—cautions; confused; easy going; mild; shallow; unambitious.

   (d) Psychological interests—apathetic; considerate; peaceable; retiring; serious; unassuming.

   (e) Flexibility—insightful; rebellious; touchy; assertive; humorous: informal.

3. The underachievers were aware of their academic weaknesses and also of possible reasons for these weaknesses.

4. More underachievers than achievers believed that they were misunderstood by their teachers.

5. Fewer underachievers than achievers believed that they were living up to the expectations of their parents.

6. The underachievers were not as sure of their future educational plans as were the achievers. (16:96-97)

John Louis Snellgrove (1960) studied the relationship between personal and socio-economic factors and underachievement of Junior and Senior high school students. Subjects for the study were selected by determining the scores on the Primary Mental Abilities Test, and through statistical procedures, comparing these scores to grade point averages on major subjects. Two hundred and thirteen pupils were selected as the sample.

A student was classified as an underachiever when there was a 1.25 standard deviations difference between Grade Point Average (GPA) in Major subjects and Primary Mental Ability (PMA) scores Tools used were: (1) California Test of Personality, (2) Fields of Study Motivation Record and (3) A Questionnaire.

The following eight hypotheses were formulated in the study: (1) There are more males who are underachievers than are females. (2) Underachievers motivated in certain academic subjects have higher grades in those subjects (3) Underachievers have personality disorders which are characteristic of this group of individuals. (4) Personality disorders which are prevalent in underachievers, if there are such disorders, gradually become increased from the seventh through the 12th grades. (50 Individuals who can plan careers in school will be less likely to under-achieve than those who do not set up this goal. (6) Underachievers rationalize the reasons for and often do not know such reasons for their underachievement. (7) Underachievers identify more with other underachievers than they do with individuals outside this group. (8) An individual who sets up an occupational goal earlier in school will be less likely to underachieve than one who does not set up this goal.

Conclusions drawn from the above hypotheses were:

(1) The above stated hypothesis is accepted at the 0.01 level of confidence, which indicates that there is a larger number of males who are underachievers than females. (a) When grades 7-12 were separated into 2 levels (7-9 and 10-12) it was found that there was a slightly higher percentage of females than males at level 7-9. (b) It was also found that there was a higher number of underachievers at the 7-9 level than at the 10-12 level. (2) A positive biserial correlation was found to exist between grades and scores on the motivation test, areas of the test consisting of questions to measure motivation in art. English, foreign language, mathematics, science, physical education, vocational education, music, history and social studies. (3) The underachievers scored below the

CTP test norms on personal, social and total adjustment, the difference between medians being significant for males and females combined or separated at the 0.01 level of confidence. (4) The reverse of the above was found to be true i.e., personality maladjustments actually decreased in underachievers, as a group from the 7th through the 12th grades. (5) There was a no significant difference between responses of underachievers and those of a control group on the questionnaire, except for combined 7-9 and 10-12 females, a lower percentage of females in the underachiever group planning on attending college. (6) There was no significant difference between males and females of the control and underachiever groups. (7) No significant differences were found. (8) significant difference were found between underachievers and the control group. (14:1859)

Arlyn Hochberg Miller (1965) Conducted a study on personality differences in achieving, underachieving and overachieving higher secondary students. It was hypothesized that differences in personality might exist in different subgroups defined in terms of the achievement.

Sample consisted of eleventh grade public high school students. Five groups were formed: achievers, underachievers, overachievers, reluctant learners and willing students. Classification was based on the discrepancy between student's actual scholastic achievement, in terms of achievement test scores and Grade Point Averages, and predictions made for them based on their measured ability. The Runner Studies of Attitude Patterns—college form, was administered to all the students to investigate personality differences.

The findings of the study were:

1. Willing students showed significantly more respect for culturally 'right' rules, respect for authority, and less inclination to question established customs and doctrines than reluctant learners and overachievers.

2. Willing students were significantly different from all other groups in regard to 'life style'. They showed the most need for certainty, and were the most structured, cautions, and tradition conscious of all groups.

3. Overachievers appeared to have a greater need to explore and experiment than achievers and willing students. They appeared to derive more satisfaction from and showed a greater desire for mental stimulation and learning than Achievers and willing students.

4. Results indicate that broad classification based on a single objective measure of achievement is an inadequate method of studying scholastic achievement in relation to personality difference. An objective measure, such as a standardized achievement test, should also be a criterion. Because of the personality differences within the broad categories of 'underachiever' and 'overachiever' suggested by the findings, reluctant learner and willing student should be added to traditional categories. (8:4454)

Srivastava (1967) investigated the factors related to educational underachievement. Four separate groups of under, over, high and low achievements with 150 pupils in each were formed out of a random sample. One thousand eight hundred and thirty seven male pupils studying in class X and XI of nine secondary and higher secondary schools on the basis of their scores on verbal and non-verbal tests of intelligence, serving as the predictor variable and average of examination marks spread over six consecutive examinations, serving as criterion variable. These groups are then compared in respect of the scores obtained by them on measures of variables viz., study habits, reading ability, academic motivation and personality characteristics. In addition to a large number of background factors. The data were analysed using product-moment correlation, analysis of variance, t-test, Chi-square and Phi-coefficient of correlation.

The findings of the study were:

1. Underachievement was related to (a) poor study habits (b) poor reading ability, which included, poor reading speed, vocabulary and spelling (c) low academic motivation (d) poor health (e) poor social and emotional adjustment and (f) problems concerning family and schools.
2. Underachievement was related to various background and personal factors like age, socio-economic status, father's profession, size of the family, number of sibling, birth order, reading interests, failure in school examination and participation in games and sports.
3. No significant relation was found to exist between underachievement and intactness of parental structure, hobbies, interest in games, sports, music and attitude towards school. (15:348)

In a comparative study of over and underachievers, **Bhaduri (1971)** wanted to find out the similarities and differences between the overachieving and underachieving students with respect to sex, grade and academic course and to make a comparison between the 2 groups. Over several psychological characteristics, comparison of the over and underachievers was made with respect to 26 psychological characteristic selected from three non-cognitive areas viz., personality—temperamental, interest-motivational and environmental-biographical.

The sample for the study was drawn from X and XI grades of the higher secondary schools. The tools used in the study were: (1) Reasoning and Numerical Ability Sbtests of Differential Aptitude Test (DAT) (2) The Junior-Senior high school personality questionnaire—Cattell and Beleft (3) The Kuder Preferences Record (vocational form) (4) A forced choice questionnaire developed by Mukherjee (5) A study habit questionnaire prepared by Jammur and (6) A biographical data schedule developed by the investigator.

In analyzing the data, examination marks and aptitude test scores were converted into T-scores and 'r's and multiple 'R's were computed. Regression equations were established and 't' test was applied for testing the hypotheses.

The major findings of the study were as follows:

1. A variable wise comparison showed a certain degree of stability in neurcticism and anxiety, overachievers tended to be less neurotic and less anxious than underachievers.
2. The group difference was in favour of the overachievers on social service and out door interest, whereas musical interest and achievement motivation of this group were found to be lower than those of their underachieving peers.
3. The overachievers showed higher scores on study habits, attitude to school and religious cultural background.
4. The underachievers, on the contrary, tended to have a higher Socio-economic status, a more congenial home condition and more of leisure time activities. (3:343)

Menon (1973) aimed at finding out the relationship existing between underachievement and some of the personality characteristics like social activity, extroversion-introversion, tolerance, mal-adjustments and masculinity-femininity and some motivational traits like academic interest, general ambition, persistence and endurance, and areas of interest like out door, aesthetic, scientific, mechanical, persuasive, clerical and social service. The hypotheses tested were;

(i) There are significant differences between the superior ability over and underachieving groups in personality characteristics, motivational traits and interest patterns; and

(ii) There are significant differences between the two groups in Socio-Economic Status (SES) and other variables selected.

The sample consisted of 1900 students. Over and underachieving groups of students were selected through stratified random sampling, giving proportionate weight to rural and urban, boys and girls and co-educational schools. The tools used were: (1) General Mental Ability Test—verbal Form A and B (2) the personality inventory (3) the motivational inventory (4) the interest inventory; and (5) a general data questionnaire, and SSLC public examination marks were taken as a measure for the academic achievement of the subjects.

The results revealed that:

(i) Overachieving groups of boys and girls of superior ability as well as the general group were found to be less extrovert and maladjusted while overachieving boys of the general group were found to be less socially active and masculine.

(ii) Overachieving groups of boys and girls of superior ability as well as the general group were found to show greater academic interests and endurance; overachieving girls from general group and overachieving boys of both groups were also found to have greater general ambition; overachievers of high ability as well as general groups showed that their persistence was greater.

(iii) Overachieving girls of the general group showed stronger interest than underachievers in aesthetic, social and mechanical activities and less interest in outdoor, persuasive and clerical activities; overachieving boys of the general group had more interest in aesthetic

activity and less interest in outdoor work, while high ability overachievers among boys had an interest in mechanical activities; and

(iv) Overachievement and underachievement were found to be influenced by socio-economic and demographic characteristics. (7:350-351)

Chaudhari, V.P. Jain (1975) made a critical study of the factors contributing to academic underachievement. It was assumed that the factors such as study habits, personality structure and environmental conditions were interrelated. For determining the various groups of underachievers, the P.S.M. General intelligence test scores and achievement of students of the last three annual examination marks were considered. Using these scores. Accomplishment Quotient (A.Q.) was calculated. The students whose critical ratio of achievement was 0.70 or below were categorized as underachievers. CR above 0.91 were grouped as bright achievers and those between 0.71 and 0.90 were called dull achievers. The other tests used were—Sinha's Anxiety Scale, Adjustment Inventory (Saxena).Study Habits Inventory (Jammur), Aronson's Graphic Expression Test and Social-Economic Status Scale (modified form—Kuppuswamy.)

The major findings of the study were: (1) the study habits of the achievers differed significantly from underachievers (2) a correlation between the study habit score and the index of achievement was quite high in the case of male candidates (3) achievement motivation of bright achievers was higher than that of bright underachievers (4) Dull achievers had low achievement motivation than bright underachievers (5) achievers who had a high level of achievement motivation had minimum anxiety where as dull achievers with low level of achievement had high level of anxiety (6) girls had higher achievement motivation (7) bright children normally came from families where parents had higher level of education (8) bright achieving female candidates had better general adjustment. (4:660)

Shanta Kumari Agarwal (1976) conducted a study to understand the phenomenon of underachievement of the higher secondary students of Rajasthan.

The objectives of the study were:

(i) To identify the relationship that might be existing between

(a) Personality and academic achievement (b) Values of the students and academic achievement (c) Parents values and academic achievement (d) SES of the family and academic achievement and (e) to study the influence of rural-urban factors on academic achievement.

The sample of 180 underachievers and 220 overachievers were selected from class XI of Rajasthan state. The tools used in the study were:

(a) Jalota's Verbal Group Test of General Mental Ability (b) Hindi version of Cattell's Junior-Senior HSPQ (c) Students values scale (d) Parent' values scales (e) Socio-economic status index (f) Dr. Bhatnagar's Attainment test in Hindi, Maths, Social Studies and General Science.

The findings of the study were:

(a) Underachievers in comparison with overachievers were less emotionally mature, less calm, less placid, less prone to getting into difficulties, less able to face reality, possessing less ego strength, less conscious, less preserving, less staid, less rule bounded, less ordered, less responsible, having weak super ego, less adventuresome, less socially bold, less disciplined and having poorer self-concept and self-control.

(b) Urban underachieves were more excitable, more impatient, more overactive, more jealous, more tense and more frustrated in comparison with rural underachievers.

(c) Rural underachievers were relatively more individualistic, more doubting, more obstructive,

more reflective, more internally restrained and more unwilling to act than urban underachievers.

(d) Rural overachievers were more outgoing, more warm-hearted, more easy going, more participating, more trustful, more adoptive and more social.

(e) Urban overachievers were more apprehensive, more worrying, more depressed, more troubled, more moody, more controlled, more socially precise, more self disciplined, more compulsive and have more self concept and self control than rural overachievers.

(f) Overachievers have stronger educational, social and humanistic values than underachievers.

(g) The parents' values were also related to the academic achievement of their children. The parents of overachievers and urban overachievers are more interested in the education and social life of their children than the parents' of underachievers and rural underachievers.

(h) Socio-economic status of parents of underachievers and overachievers was related to their achievement. (1:311-316)

Ghuman (1976) undertook a study of aptitudes, personality traits and achievement motivation of academic overachievers and underachievers with the following objectives:

(i) To find out the difference in the aptitudes, personality traits and achievement motivation of overachieving and underachieving students with regard to sex, academic streams and residential background.

(ii) To hierarchically present the relative contribution of the identified personality traits, aptitudes and levels of achievement

motivation to the prediction of academic achievement of over and underachievers, and

(iii) To find out the relationship between the personality traits, aptitudes and levels of achievement motivation of the overachievers and underachievers.

The sample of the study consisted of 1,948 students of both sexes, studying in grades IX, X and XI of the various high schools of Raipur district of Madhya Pradesh opting for different academic streams, namely Humanities, Science and Commerce. The under and the overachievers were identified on the basis of scores obtained on the Group test of general mental ability (Mehrotra) and the achievement records of the past three consecutive examinations. Finally 291 overachievers and 236 underachievers were identified. The tools used were the Scientific Aptitude Test Battery (Agarwal). Verbal Aptitude Test (Sharma), the 14 Personality Factor (PF) Test (HSPQ) and Achievement Motivation Inventory (Mehta). The statistical techniques used for data analysis were multiple coefficients, 't' test, analysis of variance and regression equations.

The findings of the investigation were:

(i) The overachievers and underachievers did not differ significantly on aptitudes, achievement motivation or personality traits.

(ii) The overachievers regardless of sex possessed high achievement motivation where as the underachievers possessed relatively low achievement motivation.

(iii) The male overachievers scored significantly higher than the male underachievers on factors G.H.I and Q3 of HSPQ where as female overachievers and underachievers differed significantly on factor C of personality on which the underachievers scored higher than the overachievers.

(iv) The greatest source of variance for the overachievers was the personality variables where as it was aptitude for the underachievers.

(v) Overachievement was primarily determined by the non-intellective personality variables where as underachievement was closely related to the intellective factors. (5:664)

Sushila Tandon (1977) studied the relationship of psychological and ecological factors to underachievement. The following were the objectives of the study: (a) to study the personality characteristics of the underachievers (b) to study the anxiety level of the underachievers (c) to study the home environment of the underachievers (d) to study the nature of relationship between personality traits and scholastic achievement among the underachievers (e) to study the nature of relationship between home environment and scholastic achievement of the underachievers.

The sample consisted of 200 students of class X who had failed in the high school examination and had an IQ of 110 or above. For the purpose of comparison another parallel group of 200 students who also had an IQ of 110 or above but had secured first division at the same examination were selected from the respective intermediate colleges. The tools used were: (a) Joshi's Test of General Mental ability (b) The 16 PF questionnaire by Cattell (c) Anxiety scale by Sinha (d) Home Environment Scale by Jain, (e) A general information blank for class teachers to give their opinion about students attendance, interest in studies, health, friends circle, leisure time activities etc. (f) A data sheet for gathering information about subject's parents academic qualification, profession, income, subjects, caste, number of siblings and their ordinal positions.

The important conclusions of the study psychological factor wise were as follows:

(i) The male group of underachievers display the following personality characteristics: easy going

and outgoing, emotionally less stable, low in frustration, tolerance, shy, apt to inferiority feeling, diffident, pessimistic, moody, depressed and highly anxious.

(ii) The male underachievers were not diligent, take less interest in studies, spend their time in roaming about and gossiping, not obedient and regular in attendance and do not have sophisticated friend's circle.

(iii) The female group of underachievers were pessimistic, harsh, assertive and highly anxious. They were not diligent, take less interest in studies, spend more time in roaming about and have less sophisticated friends.

The ecological factor wise conclusions were:

(i) The physical, emotional and socio-economic conditions of the male group of underachievers were not wholesome. Their parents were academically less qualified, have professions which are less remunerative, and have large families.

(ii) The home environment has not been found to be a relevant factor in the underachievement of the female underachievers. (17:216-220)

Sharma (1978) studied with the objective of finding out the personality attributes of the under graduates who failed to make academic achievement to their expected level of academic achievement. The variables under study were academic achievement, intelligence, socio-economic status, needs, adjustment, self-concept, interests, traits, study habits, level of aspiration and motivation.

A sample of 1000 students was drawn by stratified random sampling procedure. The application of regression equation of academic achievement on intelligence resulted in 177 underachievers (146 males and 31 females: 112 urban and 65 rural). The variables were measured using: (a) the Cattell's intelligence test scale – 3 Form A. (b) the Sharma's socio-economic status scale (c) the Bhatnagar's adapted version of Edward personal preference schedule (d) the Chatterjee's Non-language preference records (e) the Cattell's 16 PF questionnaire (f) the Rastogi's study habit inventory (g) the Ansari's level of aspiration test and (h) the Dole achievement motivation scale. The product moment correlation and analysis of variance were used to analyse the data.

The findings of the study were as follows:

(i) The more the personality needs, viz., exhibition, autonomy, affiliation, succorance, nurturance, endurance and order were frustrated, the more the chances of an under graduate becoming and underachievers.

(ii) Withdrawal, inferiority and emotional instability were the three behavioural characteristics, which were found to contribute significantly to academic underachievement.

(iii) Three interest areas namely, agriculture, crafts and out door sports contribute significantly to academic underachievement.

(iv) Personality traits namely, sizothymic, threctia, acetia, guilt, proneness, low integration, high ergic tension contributed significantly to academic underachievement.

(v) Study habits and socio-economic status were found to be associated with underachievement.

(vi) Unrealistic level of aspiration adversely affected the academic achievement. (13:357)

Jahan (1985) in his study compared the personality profiles of over and underachieving students studying in science, arts and commerce streams in pre-university classes. The sample comprised of 758 male and female students. Cattel's high school personality questionnaire (HSPQ) and a composite of marks obtained in different subjects of science, arts and commerce streams served as measures of personality and academic achievement respectively. Thorndike's method of identifying over and underachievers on the basis of discrepancies between actual achievement and that predicted on the basis of intelligence was employed. The significance of difference between the means of scores on the fourteen dimensions of HSPQ secured by the over and underachievers of the three streams was ascertained by 't' test.

The major findings were: (1) the overachievers of science stream were more reserved, intelligent, emotionally stable, excitable, obedient, sober, conscientious shy, self assured, self sufficient, controlled and relaxed as compared to the underachievers. (2) The overachievers of the arts stream were more warm-hearted intelligent affected by feelings, undemonstrative, assertive, enthusiastic, conscientious, zestful, apprehensive and tense as compared to underachievers, (3) The overachievers of the commerce stream were more reserved, intelligent, affected by feelings, sober, conscientious and self assured as compared to the underachievers. (6:827)

Puri (1987) made a detailed study of the personality traits and self-concept of the underachievers of the 16-18 years age group in the Indian context along with the socio-economic status of their families.

The sample of the study consisted of 425 students (244 boys and 181 girls) of the 16-18 years age group, who had 90 or above Percentile (PR) on the progressive matrices test and had secured less than 48 per cent marks in the high school examination. The sample was selected from 2147 class XI students of 12 intermediate colleges of Lucknow city. The tools used in the study were: (1) Kuppuswamy's socio-economic status scale (Revised edition 1981) (2) RPM test

(3) Cattell's High School Personality Questionnaire (4) Sherry, Verma and Goswami's test of self concept.

Besides these tools, the criterion of academic achievement was the marks of the high school examination. The collected data were tabulated and analysed using suitable statistical techniques.

The findings of the study were:

1. About 19.8 per cent of the intellectually gifted students did not come upto the expected level of academic performance.
2. The majority of the underachievers belonged to lower SES groups and had proper self-concept.
3. The underachievers generally tended to be warm-hearted and easy going, had comparatively lower scholastic capacity and were inactive. They tended to be assertive, aggressive, stubborn and dominant, were impulsive, lively happy go-lucky and gay persons, and tended to be socially bold. They were generally overprotected, sensitive, individualistic and reflective and were found to be apprehensive, worrying and troubled.
4. The underachiever girls tended to be more group-dependent, and were generally tense, over wrought and frustrated. (11:845)

Terry, Patricia Ann Simpson (1994) undertook a study of self esteem in underachieving students reported that students who are underachievers present a perplexing problem to educators from the standpoint of implementing appropriate motivational and counselling strategies. Science underachievement is one of the indicators of the at risk student, and understanding of the factors contributing to underachievement may prove critical to dropout prevention.

The purpose of this study was to investigate the level of self esteem in underachieving and achieving student in a population of at-risk secondary students. In addition to achievement level, two other independent variables, gender and grade level, were utilized in the higher order, non equivalent groups research design. Underachieving and achieving male and female students from grades 10, 11, and 12 equally divided as to achievement level and gender, were administered the school form of the cooper smith self-esteem inventories.

A 2 × 2 × 3 (underachievers, achievers; male, female; grades 10, 11, 12) factorial design was used in analyzing the data from the SEI. Results revealed no statistically significant 3-way or 2-way interactions among the independent variables. There was a statistically significant main effect difference for the variable achievement level. For students who underachieve, the mean score on the cooper smith SEI was significantly lower than the mean score of students who achieve in educational settings. The eta-squared value was 0.09 findings are discussed in light of the characteristics peculiar to the population. The utility of global self-esteem scores versus dimension—specific scores is also discussed. (18:1899A).

Yaworski, Jo Ann (1996) conducted a study to know why underachieving college students succeed or fail and reported that: Through the use of qualitative and quantitative research methods, a grounded theory was built to explain successful and unsuccessful behaviour among underachieving high income college students. Twenty one "at-risk" students and twelve of their professor participated in 2 one hour in-depth interviews in which data were audio taped and transcribed verbatim. They also completed a 119 item survey which was constructed from the interview questions and served as a quantitative "check " on the qualitative data.

It was found that students possessed and created systems of attributes and behaviours which either worked in favour or against academic success. These system were directly linked to four layers of constructs: the individual, the family and peers, the education institution as represented by professors, and the society at large. Intrinsic motivation, long term goals, self efficacy, self-regulation, strategic effort, and a belief in incremental intelligence comprised the high achieving students' theory of success. In accordance with motivational theories, the low achieving students believed that intelligence was static and that inherent ability was a determining factor for success in school. Therefore, they worked far below their academic potential, by placing social activity as a priority over academia.

Five major conclusions were drawn: (1) students become successful in college if they are inspired by long term goals that are connected with college study (2) students who attribute success to strategic effort are more apt to succeed in college than students who attribute success to ability (3) study strategies instruction is useful to students who are intrinsically motivated but may not be effective with students who are extrinsic motivated (4) students are more apt to become successful in college if they perceive they have strong parental social support (5) qualitative methods are useful in predicting which "at-risk" students will become successful. (19:1543A)

Yu, Shirley Lynn (1996) in his empirical studies on cognitive strategy use and motivation in underachieving students reported that—underachieving students perform more poorly on academic measures than what is expected of them based on their ability. The first empirical study examined the relations of self-competence, strategy use on a memory task, and achievement for 68 middle and high school students identified as underachieving or learning disabled and comparison students achieving at grade level. ANOVAs showed that students identified as underachieving and learning disabled reported lower cognitive self-competence than did comparison students. The learning disabled students indicated lower social and general self-competence, as well as poorer performance and use of less sophisticated strategies on the memory task than did comparison and underachieving students. Regressions showed that type of strategy used was the best predictor of performance on the task, and group membership did not predict achievement, cluster analysis indicated that there were intra-individual differences in the patterns of motivational and cognitive variables that cut across the a priori groups of children.

The second empirical study examined the self-reported motivational and cognitive correlates of achievement of 603 college chemistry student's particularly for female and minority students who earned lower grades in the course than their classmates. Regressions showed that the motivational and cognitive variables helped explain grade beyond gender or ethnic group membership. Underachievers tended not to be strategic or to endorse adaptive motivational beliefs, while overachievers seemed to compensate for their low aptitude with greater strategy use and adaptive motivational beliefs.

The findings provide evidence for the importance of cognitive and motivational variables in models of student learning and suggest a need to reconsider the construct of underachievement (20:4652A)

Review Related to Causes of Underachievement in Biology

Pal and Saxena (1970) have conducted research with the objectives of determining the extent, range and nature of problems of over, under and normal achieving students and to probe into their study habits, self-concept, attitudes, interests, and future vocational plans. The study was conducted on a random sample of 305 students from Biology curriculum and 517 from Mathematics curriculum. The 3 groups were identified on the basis of the ability scores on the Joshi's test of mental ability and the B.Sc., part-I achievement scores. Those of average ability and below average in achievement were regarded as underachievers. Those who had achievement commensurate with their mental ability were designated as normal achievers. Interview schedules for under and overachievers and teachers, the Mooney's problem check list and a Hindi adaptation of the Brown and Holtzman's survey of study habits and attitudes were used for collection of data.

The analysis revealed that the underachievers had higher level problems, interested in out door games, more concern over finances, future vocational and educational plans, looked more for personal help from the teachers, and were more inclined to be members of political parties as compared to overachievers. On the other hand, overachievers marked higher in problems of health and physical development. They possessed better study habits, study hours, attitude towards school, teachers, peers and studies, whereas normal achievers possessed more positive attitude towards studies, peers, school and teachers; their reading interest was high in detective stories and they participated more in social activities.

As regards the Biology curriculum sample, the underachiever identified numerically more problems in areas of finance, living conditions and employment, future vocational and educational plans. Study hours, study habits and self-concept did not influence underachievement.

As regards the Mathematics curriculum sample in universities, the underachiever showed more concern over finances, living conditions and employment; they also had more problems in areas of adjustment to college work. Study hours, attitudes and self-concept did not contribute to the underachievement of the group. (10:336-337)

Saxena (1972) undertook an investigation to discover the differences between the over and underachievers with respect to their interest, need patterns and adjustment problems, study habits, and personal and background factors.

Sample of 1769 boys of class XI of age group 15 and above was drawn using the cluster sampling method of randomly selected class sections. They belonged to Mathematics, Biology, Commerce and Arts streams. The over, normal and underachievers were identified using a multiple regression equation for each curriculum separately. The following instruments were used to investigate the problem: (1) Joshi's Group Test of Intelligence (2) SPM) (3) Chatterji's Non-Language preference record (4) Edward's personal preference schedule (5) Saxena's Vayakthitva Parakh Prasnavali (6) Mooney problem check list (7) Holtzman and Brown's survey of study habits and attitudes (8) Personal data schedule.

The aggregate marks obtained at the high school examination of the Uttar Pradesh Board were used as the criterion measure.

Some of the important findings were as follows:

1. The overachievers were associated with aspiration for higher achievement, lower number of problems of adjustment, better study habits, better health status, longer study hours, positive attitude towards school, study, peers and school work, positive self-concept.

2. The underachievers were meek, submissive, timid, brooding, impulsive and dependent type of immature individuals. They were associated with greater number of problems, poor study habits, over aged, shorter study hours and lack of self-concept (12:258-265)

Nair Sankaran (1987) undertook a study on factors related to underachievement in Biology with the following objectives. (1) to find out the effect of the selected personality variables on underachievement in Biology students of secondary schools. (2) to find out whether there is any significant difference in the proportion of underachievers or any of the other related levels of achievers in Biology when extreme groups are taken on the basis of intelligence, and (3) to find out whether there is any significant difference in the proportion of underachievers in

Biology when extreme groups are taken on the basis of any one of the social variables selected for the study.

The study was confined to Malayalam medium students of standard IX from selected secondary schools. The regression technique was employed to classify the sample into overachievers, normal achievers and underachievers with two intelligence measures and a standardized achievement test in Biology.

The following tools were used to collect the data: (1) Kerala University verbal group test of intelligence and Kerala University nonverbal group test of intelligence. (2) Achievement test in Biology. (3) Scale of attitude towards science, scientists, problem solving and academic work. (4) The Calicut university adjustment inventory. (5) General data sheet—to gather data regarding social variables. Comparisons were made with the help of two tailed tests of significance for differences between mean using the formula for critical ratio.

The findings of the study were: (1) Attitudinal variables are most effective in discrimination between underachievers, normal achievers and overachievers in Biology at secondary school. (2) All the eight attitudinal and adjust mental variables are able to discriminate between groups of the 3 achievement pairs, namely overachievers and normal achievers, normal achievers and underachievers, overachievers and underachievers. (3) a) low intelligence is related to underachievement in Biology b) Incidence of underachievement is higher among boys than girls c) The incidence of underachievement is greater among the subjects of high age group d) Incidence of underachievement is greater among backward castes e) Incidence of underachievement is related to the size of the family to which the student belongs f) The incidence of underachievement is greater among the students of government schools than private schools g) Rural residence of child also facilitates the incidence of underachievement h) Education of parents shows a profound influence on underachievement. i) Better SES will lead to better achievement motivation. (4) Out of the 16 social variables, seven variables such as age of the subjects, educational status of father, professional status of father, income status of father and educational status of siblings (elder members) were seen to be associated with all the 3 achievement levels (overachievers, normal achievers and underachievers). (9)

The above review of related literature has helped the researcher in getting clear ideas about the methodology which could be followed including selection and size of the sample, choosing appropriate variables, tools for collection of data and the appropriate statistical techniques. In most of the previous studies the researchers have developed regression equation using intelligence and achievement test scores to classify the sample into under, normal and overachievers. Hence, the researcher decided to use regression equation for classifying the students into under, normal and overachievers. For testing the significance of the hypotheses, many researchers have used product moment correlation and analysis of variance. In the present study also, the same techniques have been used. The detailed description of these techniques has been presented in the chapter to follow.

The findings of the previous studies have given an insight into the factors responsible for and the characteristics of under and overachievers. According to these studies, underachievers are characterized by poor study habits low achievement motivation, low academic motivation, poor social and emotional adjustment, high anxiety, low socio-economic status poor health less emotionally mature, less clam, less placid, possessing less ego-strength, less conscious, less preserving, less rule bounded, less ordered, less responsible, having weak super ego, less adventure-some, less socially bold, less disciplined and having poorer self-concept and self-control. Whereas overachievers possessed better study habits, study hours, positive attitude towards school, teachers, peers and studies, were associated with aspiration for higher achievement, better health status, positive self concept, high achievement motivation. They were more outgoing, more warm-hearted, more participating, more trustful, more adaptive and more social. Overachievers tended to be less neurotic and less anxious than underachievers.

This information has made the researcher to know more about the factors which contribute to underachievement so that the results may help teachers, parents and others interested in the cause of education. It has become possible to come up with specific recommendations by providing justification based on the present study and also keeping in view the total perspective of studies in this area.

It is evident from the above review quoted in section 1 and 2 that a number of studies have been conducted on the causes of academic underachievement, but a very few studies (i.e., three only) on the causes of underachievement in Biology. However the coverage of causal factors is not that comprehensive. It may be added here that, studies having bearing on the present investigation were found to be almost conspicuous by their absence. As such, the present study is undertaken with a view to identify the factors causing underachievement in Biology covering more relevant causal factors.

REFERENCES

1. Agarwal, Shanta Kumari, "A Psycho-social Study of Academic Underachievement". University of Rajasthan, 1976. *Indian Dissertation Abstracts,* 10, 3 and 4, July-Dec. 1981, pp. 311-316.

2. Armstrong, Marion Elizabeth. "A Comparison of the Interests and Social Adjustment of Underachievers and Normal Achievers at the Secondary Level". The university of Connecticut, 1955. *Dissertation Abstracts International,* 15, 8, Aug. 1955, pp. 1349-1350.

3. Bhaduri, A. "Comparative Study of Certain Psychological Characteristics of the Over and the Underachievers in Higher

Secondary Schools". Calcutta University, 1971. In Buch, M.B. (Ed.), *Second Survey of Research in Education (1972-78)* Baroda: Society for Educational Research and Development, 1979.

4. Chaudhari, V.P. Jain. "Factors Contributing to Academic Underachievement". Nagpur University, 1975. In Buch, M.B. (Ed.), *Third Survey of Research in Education (1978-1983).* New Delhi: N.C.E.R.T., 1986.

5. Ghuman, M.S. "A Study of Aptitudes, Personality Traits and Achievement Motivation of Academic Overachievers and Underachievers". Rohtak University, 1976. In Buch, M.B. (Ed.), *Third Survey of Research in Education (1978-1983),* New Delhi: N.C.E.R.T., 1986.

6. Jahan. Q. "A Study of Personality Profiles of Students of Science, Arts and Commerce at the Higher Secondary Level of Education in Relation to their Academic Achievement". Aligarh Muslim University, 1985. In Buch, M.B. (Ed.), *Fourth Survey of Research in Education (1983-1988)* Vol. 1. New Delhi: N.C.E.R.T., 1991.

7. Menon, S.K. "A Comparative Study of the Personality Characteristics of Overachievers and Underachievers of High Ability". Kerala University, 1973. In Buch, M.B. (Ed.), *Second Survey of Research in Education,* Baroda: Society for Educational Research and Development, 1979.

8. Miller, Arlyn Hochberg. "A Study of Personality Differences of Achieving and Underachieving Eleventh Grade Students". Temple University, 1965. *Dissertation Abstracts International,* 26, 8, Feb. 1966, p. 4454.

9. Nair, Sankaran, C.K. *Factors Related to Underachievement in Biology of Secondary School Students.* Unpublished Doctoral Dissertation, University of Calicut, 1987.

10. Pal, S.K., and Saxena P.C. "The Problems of Over, Under and Normal Achieving College Students". Department of Education, Allahabad University, 1970. (N.C.E.R.T. financed) In Buch, M.B. (Ed.), *A Survey of Research in Education.* Baroda: Centre of Advanced Studies in Education, 1974.

11. Puri, K. "Personality Traits and Self Concept of 16-18 years old Underachievers". Avadh University, 1987. In Buch, M.B. (Ed.), *Fourth Survey of Research in Education (1983-88).* Vol. 1, New Delhi: N.C.E.R.T., 1991.

12. Saxena, P.C. "A Study of Interests, Need Patterns and Adjustment Problems of Over and Underachievers". Allahabad University, 1972. *Indian Dissertation Abstracts.* 17, July-Sept. 1988, pp. 258-265.

13. Sharma, G.S. "Attributes of Underachieving Undergraduate Students". Meerut University, 1978. In Buch, M.B. (Ed.), *Second Survey of Research in Education.* Baroda: Society for Educational Research and Development, 1979.

14. Snellgrove, John Louis. "A Study of Relationships between Certain Personal and Socio-Economic Factors and Underachievement". University of Albana, 1960. *Dissertation Abstracts International,* 21, 7, Jan. 1961, p. 1859.

15. Srivastava, A.K. "An Investigation into the Factors Related to Educational Underachievement". Patna University, 1967. In Buch, M.B. (Ed.), *A Survey of Research in Education,* Baroda: C.A.S.E., 1974.

16. Stoner, William Gerald. "Factors Related to the Underachievement of High School Students". Stanford University, 1956. *Dissertation Abstracts International,* 17, 1, Jan. 1957, pp. 96-97.

17. Tandon, Sushila, "A Psychological and Ecological Study of Underachievers". Banaras Hindu University, 1977. *Indian Dissertation Abstracts,* Jan.-Dec. 1985, pp. 216-220.

18. Terry, Patricia Ann Simpson. "A Study of Self-esteem in Underachieving Students is a Population of At-Risk Secondary Students". The University of Mississippi, 1994. *Dissertation Abstracts International,* 55, 7, Jan. 1995, p. 1899-A.

19. Yaworski, Jo Ann, "Why Students Succeed or Fail: Theories of Underachieving Affluent College Students". State University of New York at Albany, 1996. *Dissertation Abstracts International,* 57, 4, Oct. 1996, p. 1543-A.

20. Yu, Shirely Lynn, "Cognitive Strategy use and Motivation in Underachieving Students". The University of Michigan, 1996. *Dissertation Abstracts International,* 57, 11, May 1997, p. 4652-A.

3

Methodology of the Study

In the previous chapter, a review of related literature and studies on various aspects of over, normal and underachievers in relation to various causal factors has been presented. This chapter presents the methodology adopted by the researcher in the present study. It includes the statement of the problem, selection of variables, discussion and definitions, and variables and terms, identification of over, normal and underachievers, hypotheses formulated, description of tools used for collection of data, sampling, administration and scoring of the tests and statistical techniques used for analysis of data.

Statement of the Problem

The problem of the present study is —*"An investigation into the Factors Causing Underachievement in Biology among the First Year Pre-university Students of Chitradurga District"*.

Selection of Variables

A variable is that factor which is measured, manipulated and observed by investigator (Tuckman, 1978). The variables involved in the present study are:

(i) Independent variable and (ii) Dependent variable.

Independent Variable

An independent variable is a factor, which is measured, manipulated, observed and selected by the investigator for the purpose of determining its relationship to an observed phenomena. (37:58-59) The independent variables considered by the investigator in the present study were:

1. Attitude towards science
2. Achievement motivation
3. Study habits
4. Adjustment
5. Comprehensive anxiety
6. Self concept
7. Socio-economic status

Dependent Variable

A dependent variable is the one which is measured and observed by the investigator to determine the effect of independent variable on it. (37:58-59) The dependent variable considered by the investigator in the present study was—achievement in Biology.

Predictor Variable

The predictor variable in the present study was intelligence. Achievement may be predicted on the basis of intelligence. Intelligence test scores and achievement scores are used to predict the level of achievement of a student with a given I.Q. This is predicted with the help of regression, when the actual achievement score is different from the predicted score, the predicted score is used as the basis for categorising students into over, normal and underachievers.

Discussions and Definitions of Variables and Terms

(1) Under, normal and overachievers

The term 'underachievers' has come to mean a student who appears to possess the ability to achieve a considerably higher grade than his present record shows. In other words, underachievers are those who show a discrepancy between their potential and actual achievements.

According to the Education Commission underachievers consist of children who are not intellectually dull but are at least of average and may even be of superior ability. (12:427-428). This definition suffers from the fact that it conforms the incidence of underachievement to average and higher intelligence levels. However, modern psychological literature gives the term a broad connotation by considering it as existing at all levels of intelligence. Underachievement would, therefore stand for a level of achievement which is considerably below an individual's potential for achievement as measured by conventional scholastic aptitude tests.

According to the 'Dictionary of Psychological and Psycho-analytic Terms (English & English 1965)', an underachiever is a person who does not perform in specified ways as well as expected from certain known characteristics or previous records, specially a student who does not accomplish as much in school as would be expected from his measured intelligence. Achievement is considered to be mostly dependent on the intellectual capacities of an individual.

Keeping this in view, in general an:

(i) Underachiever is one whose achievement is less than his intellectual capacity.

(ii) Normal achiever is one whose achievement commensurate with his abilities, and

(iii) Overachiever is one whose achievement is more than his intellectual capacity.

Different studies have defined under, normal and overachievers, depending on the focus of research and the methodology adopted.

Gowan in his study has considered a student whose performance was less than one standard deviation below his ability, as an underachiever. (13:153-167).

Tolor Alexander in his study on the incidence of underachievement has defined underachiever as a student with at least one standard error of estimate below expectancy based on his own intelligence quotient. (36:63-64).

Saxena defined underachievers as those individuals whose actual achievement falls at least one standard error of estimate below the regression line of prediction on achievement. Further he has defined overachievers as those individuals whose actual achievement falls at least one standard error of estimate above the regression line of prediction on achievement. (30:258-265).

In the present study—students who were above + 1 S.D. distance from the mean on the regression line were considered as overachievers, students who were below –1 S.D. distance from the mean were considered as underachievers. Those students who were in between ± 1 S.D. distance from the mean were considered as normal achievers.

Underachievement

It is defined as "a performance on the part of an individual student which falls below that predicted for him on the basis of an aptitude measure". (18:5235).

Science Attitude

Science attitude has been defined as a generalised attitude towards the universe of science content and being measured in terms of its favourableness or unfavourableness estimated from the scores obtained by the subjects on an attitude scale towards science. (14:2-8).

In the present study, it is used in the sense as defined by Thurstone as, "The degree of positive or negative affect associated with some psychological object". The psychological object in this case is science subject towards which students may have either positive or negative affect.

Achievement Motivation

Achievement motivation refers to predisposition to

derive satisfaction from success in competition with some standard of excellence. (Victor, 1964).

It is defined as a disposition to strive for success in competition with others with some standard of excellence, set by the individual. (Decharms, 1968).

Johnson defines it as "the impetus to do well, relative to some standard of excellence, and a person with strong need for achievement wants to be successful to some challenging task, not for the profit or status but merely for the state of doing well". (20:120)

'Achievement Motivation' is a disposition to strive for success in situations where an individual's performance is evaluated. (6:1-3).

According to Bhargava—(a) achievement motivation is a drive which can be aroused by inducing a situation of ego involvement or achievement orientation. This situation produces the same kind of effect of the subjects projection as is in the case of manipulation in hunger and sex deprivation. (b) achievement motivation varies from person to person, group to group and is open to cultural influences. Achievement motivation may be acquired through social and cultural milieu and training programmes. (c) the achievement motivation is acquired by following the same process as in the case of reward and punishment. (4:2-7).

Therefore, from the various definitions of achievement motivation, it can be considered as an inner force or psychological urge or motive in an individual to come up in life successfully. It stresses upon the individual need and desire to do well at some challenging task or an endeavour to perform better than before.

Study Habits

Study habits are typical methods practised by students to learn budgeting of study time, selecting place of study, reading methods, note-taking skill, motivation skills, improving memory, examination-taking skill, use of knowledge of results and healthy habits, which are necessary to achieve success in the examination (27:1-2).

Adjustment

Adjustment is defined as the individual's ability to have a feeling of satisfaction in the educational, social, home, health and emotional environment in which he is, and he feels most of his needs have been duly satisfied (met). (32:2-8).

Adjustment refers to healthy energetic participation in group activity, grasping of responsibility, at times to the point of leadership, and above all avoidance of any self deception in the adjusting. The well adjusted child meets his school environment with the initiative appropriate to a full sharing with others and the optimum development of himself (34:102).

Comprehensive Anxiety

"Anxiety is a response of an individual to a hidden or subjective danger; a fear of possible failure or of punishment in future". (34: 265).

'Comprehensive Anxiety', is defined as a display of anxiety reactions in different spheres of life. (33.3).

Self-concept

"Self concept is the individual's way of looking at himself. It also signifies his way of thinking, feeling and behaving". (28:3).

Self concept is defined as—"An organised configuration of perceptions of the self which are admissible to awareness. It is compared of such elements as the perceptions of one's characteristics and abilities, the percepts and concepts of self in relation to others and to the environment, the value qualities which are perceived as associated with experiences and objects, and the goals and ideals which are perceived as having positive or negative valence". (Rogers, 1951).

Socio-economic Status

Socio-economic status of an individual is a sort of rank or position as determined by the joint influence of his social and economic rankings in the society he belongs to. More precisely, it is one's place on socio-economic scale. Such status emerges in accordance with the degree of his prestige in the social structure and the slab of income he happens to earn. (21:3-11).

Identification of Under, Normal and Overachievers

Underachievement in academic subjects finds a prominent mention in contemporary research literature. However, educationists and researchers have not yet evolved any universally accepted meaning for the concept and therefore, the methods used for identification are far from satisfactory, various methods such as keen observation, interrogation and the use of the most sophisticated statistical techniques employing psychological tests and materials are used for identifying underachievers.

According to Deo, the question of identifying underachievers is not easy to answer though the concept of underachievement sounds simple encugh as that achievement which is below the level expected on the basis of intelligence. This involves two types of tasks; first, to determine what is expected of each individual and secondly, how much lower than expectation the achievement should be to be considered underachievement.

It cannot be expected that all individuals achieve upto expectations on all occasions. Some factors that affect achievement may exist at times and hence a margin must be allowed for the expected level of achievement. This implies that some deviation is possible in the case of expected achievement. Underachievement is a phenomenon that persists at all levels of achievement and therefore it can be identified by comparing the individual's achievement scores and intelligence scores. Along with the identification of underachievers, it is possible to identify normal achievers and overachievers and the classification of achievement as overachievers, normal achievers and underachievers is a matter of real concern to educational practitioners.

Farquhar and Payne (10:674-684) have discussed four different methods of identifying over, normal and underachievers. They are—

(i) Central Tendency Split Technique

Under and overachievement is determined by dichotomizing a distribution of combined aptitude and achievement measures.

Shaw and Mc Cuen (1960) used this technique, underachievers were determined by selecting individuals who had earned a grade point average that was below the class mean, but who were in the top 25 per cent of the class in ability on intelligence scale (Pintner General Ability Test, Verbal series). They did not study overachievers, Dowd (1952) employed a similar technique where he too did not identify overachievers.

(ii) Arbitrary Partitions Technique

In this, discrepancies are determined by contrasting extreme groups in achievement and aptitude distributions, and by eliminating a middle group. Shaw and Brown (1957), Shaw and Grub (1958) used arbitrary partitions technique, but studied only upper quartile in ability. Frankel (1960) used this technique but limited to the study of underachievement, whereas Brookover (1962) considered the reliability of the dependent and independent variables. However, subjects falling within a standard error above the mean on either variable were eliminated.

(iii) Relative Discrepancy Splits Technique

Grade point average and aptitude predictors are ranked independently. Under and overachievement is determined by the discrepancy between the 2 ranks.

Many studies have been conducted using this technique, an illustrative approach is that of Diener (1960), which involves converting aptitude and GPA into T-scores. The discrepant groups are then defined on the basis of difference of rank, plus and minus 15 'T' score units.

(iv) Regression Model Selection

In this technique, a regression equation is used to predict achievement from IQ measures. Under and overachievement is then determined on the basis of the discrepancy between predicted and actual achievement.

Gerberich (1941) used this method by smoothing of a scatter diagram of achievement predicted from aptitude measures. Bhaduri (1971) has identified over and underachievers by comparing their expected achievement and actual achievement in school examination marks. Abraham's (1974) studies on some factors relating to underachievement in English among secondary school pupils. The technique used for classifying over, normal and underachievers was Farquhar's method, by developing three regression equations for each instructional level, using intelligence scores as independent variable and achievement as dependent.

The knowledge of these studies has helped the researcher to determine the technique to be used for the identification and classification of over, normal and underachievers. In the present study, the researcher has used the regression model selection to identify over, normal and underachievers in order to overcome the limitations met with the other techniques. The limitations found in other techniques for identification of over, normal and underachievers are:

1. In the case of central tendency split technique, the overachievers were not identified.

2. In the arbitrary partition technique, the middle groups were eliminated, namely the normal achievers were not identified.

3. In relative discrepancy splits technique, differences in ranks were taken into consideration and actual scores were ignored.

Not only because of the limitations of other techniques but also because of the reason that many researchers like Srivastava (1967), Dhaliwal (1971), Saxena (1972), Sharma (1972), Subramania Dandapani (1977), Nair (1987), Sarojamma (1989), Shahpur (1994), Mary Suvarna (1997) have used regression equation successfully in their studies to classify over and underachievers based on the discrepancy between actual scores and predicted scores.

Since the objective of the present study is to find out the factors causing underachievement in Biology among the pre-university students, the subjects have been classified into over, normal and underachievers. In order to identify the over, the normal and the underachievers, Group intelligence test and Achievement test in Biology were administered to 480 students of first year P.U.C. studying in pre-university colleges of Chitradurga District.

Coefficient of correlation of intelligence scores with Biology achievement scores was obtained. The correlation coefficient was used to work out a regression equation with intelligence as the independent variable (X) and achievement in Biology as the dependent variable (Y).

Development of Regression Equation

A regression equation is used to predict achievement from I.Q. measures, under and overachievement is then determined on the basis of the discrepancy between predicted and actual achievement. The achievement scores in Biology are called criterion and the intelligence scores are called predictor. An equation can be developed for the prediction of the criterion from known values of the predictor variable.

If the data representing the criterion and the predictor variables are plotted, a line assumed to be satisfactory for predicting the criterion from the predictor variable is called a regression line. The mathematical equation for representing the regression line which may or may not be linear is called the regression equation.

Regression Equation with Intelligence as the Aptitudinal Criterion

X – Intelligence (DIQ) Y – Achievement in Biology (ATS)

$\bar{X}$ – 100.69 $\bar{Y}$ = 35.98 r = 0.72

S_X – 18.47 S_Y = 15.77

The regression equation of Y on X:

$\hat{Y} = [r(S_x/S_y)\ (X - \bar{X})] + \bar{Y}$ .... (17:368)

$\hat{Y} = 0.61\ X - 25.44$

The researcher has predicted the achievement scores of the students on the basis of their IQs with the use of

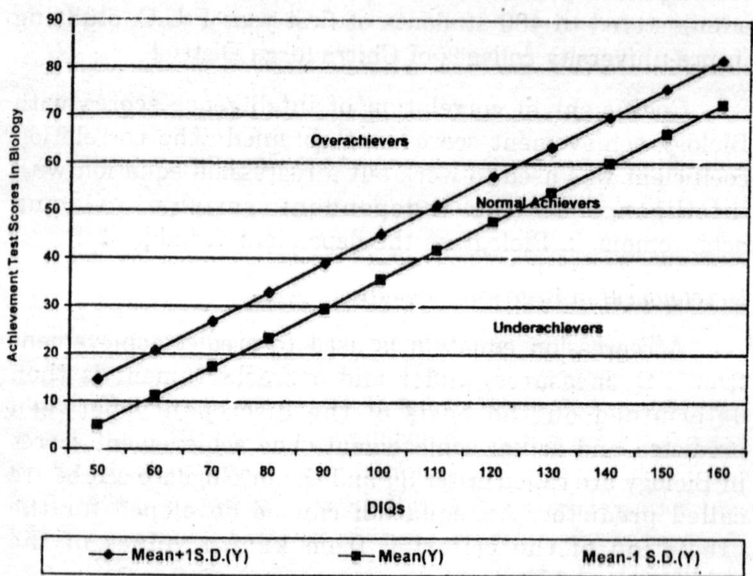

Figure 1: Identification of Overachievers, Normalachievers and Underachievers by using Regression Equation.

regression equation, the predicted achievement for each student was calculated. The difference between predicted achievement and the actual achievement was found out. The mean and standard deviation for these differences were calculated. (10:151-181). All the students who were above +1 S.D. distance from the mean on the regression line were considered as overachievers, those below -1 S.D. distance from the mean were considered as underachievers and the rest as normal achievers.

In the present study, the standard deviation for difference scores was found to be 9.5, Based on this, students were classified into over, normal and underachievers.

Table 3.1: Number of Over, Normal and Underachievers Obtained by Using Regression Equation

Sl.No.	*Group*	*No. of Students*
1	Overachievers	71
2	Normal Achievers	259
3	Underachievers	90
	Total	420

Hypotheses

Based upon the discussion of variables and also keeping in view the objectives of the study, the following research hypotheses have been formulated.

1. There is no significant difference between underachievers, normalachievers and overachievers in respect of Attitude towards science.

Sub Hypotheses

(i) There is no significant difference in the mean scores of underachievers and normal achievers in respect of Attitude towards science.

(ii) There is no significant difference in the mean scores of underachievers and overachievers in respect of attitude towards science.

(iii) There is no significant difference in the mean scores of normalachievers and overachievers in respect of Attitude towards science.

2. There is no significant difference between underachievers, normalachievers and overachievers in respect of Achievement motivation.

Sub Hypotheses

(i) There is no significant difference in the mean scores of underachievers and normalachievers in respect of Achievement motivation.

(ii) There is no significant difference in the mean scores of underachievers and overachievers in respect of Achievement motivation.

(iii) There is no significant difference in the mean scores of normalachievers and overachievers in respect of Achievement motivation.

3. There is no significant difference between underachievers, normalachievers and overachievers in respect of Study habits.

Sub Hypotheses

(i) There is no significant difference in the mean scores of underachievers and normalachievers in respect of Study habits.

(ii) There is no significant difference in the mean scores of underachievers and overachievers in respect of Study habits.

(iii) There is no significant difference in the mean scores of normalachievers and overachievers in respect of Study habits.

4. There is no significant difference between underachievers, normalachievers and overachievers in respect of Adjustment.

Sub Hypotheses

(i) There is no significant difference in the mean scores of underachievers and normalachievers in respect of Adjustment.

(ii) There is no significant difference in the mean scores of underachievers and overachievers in respect of Adjustment.

(iii) There is no significant difference in the mean scores of normalachievers and overachievers in respect of Adjustment.

5. There is no significant difference between underachievers, normalachievers and overachievers in respect of Comprehensive anxiety.

Sub Hypotheses

(i) There is no significant difference in the mean scores of underachievers and normalachievers in respect of Comprehensive anxiety.

(ii) There is no significant difference in the mean scores of underachievers and overachievers in respect of Comprehensive anxiety.

(iii) There is no significant difference in the mean scores of normalachievers and overachievers in respect of Comprehensive anxiety.

6. There is no significant difference between underachievers, normalachievers and overachievers in respect of Self concept.

Sub Hypotheses

(i) There is no significant difference in the mean scores of underachievers and normalachievers in respect of Self concept.

(ii) There is no significant difference in the mean scores of underachievers and overachievers in respect of Self concept.

(iii) There is no significant difference in the mean scores of normalachievers and overachievers in respect of Self concept.

7. There is no significant difference between underachievers, normalachievers and overachievers in respect of Socio-economic status.

Sub Hypotheses

(i) There is no significant difference in the mean scores of underachievers and normalachievers in respect of Socio-economic status.

(ii) There is no significant difference in the mean scores of underachievers and overachievers in respect of Socio-economic status.

(iii) There is no significant difference in the mean scores of normalachievers and overachievers in respect of Socio-economic status.

Description of the Tools used for the Collection of Data

Based on review of related literature and personal experience and also keeping in view the variables and the objectives of the study the investigator has used the following tools for the collection of relevant data.

1. Group Test of Intelligence (G.C. Ahuja, 1976)—English version.

2. Achievement test in Biology constructed by the researcher was used for identifying over, normal and underachievers in Biology.

The following tools were used for assessing hypothesized casual factors:

3. Science Attitude Scale (SAS) by Avinash Grewal, 1990.

4. Achievement Motive Test (ACMT) by Bhargava, 1994.

5. Palsane and Sharma Study Habits Inventory (PSSHI) by Palsane and Sadhana Sharma, 1989.
6. Adjustment Inventory for College Students (AICS) by Sinha and Singh, 1980.
7. Sinha's Comprehensive Anxiety Test (SCAT) by Sinha and Sinha, 1984.
8. Self-concept Questionnaire (SCQ) by Rajakumar Saraswat, 1984.
9. Kakkar Socio-economic Status Scale (KSESS) by Kakkar, 1993.

See appendix A to J for the tools used by the researcher.

Group Test of Intelligence (GGTI)

The tool was constructed and standardized by Ahuja, 1976. The test is meant for assessing the general mental ability of students of age group 13 to 17+ years studying in classes. VIII to XI. The test contains 8 sub tests. Test 1

Table 3.2: Number of Items and Time Limits for Each Sub Test of Group Test of Intelligence

Sl. No.	*Sub Test*	*No. of Items*	*Time Limit*
1.	Following Directions	9	4 Minutes
2.	Classification	20	4 Minutes
3.	Analogies	20	4 Minutes
4.	Arithmetic Reasoning	6	4 Minutes
5.	Vocabulary	40	4 Minutes
6.	Comprehension	8	4 Minutes
7.	Series	12	4 Minutes
8.	Best Answers	20	4 Minutes
	Total	135	32 Minutes

is an additional sub-test which is meant for practice only. The remaining seven sub tests from II to VIII are the tests proper. There are 135 test items and 24 practice examples. The total testing time for all the eight sub tests is 32 minutes and the time required for instructions and practice is approximately 35 minutes. Clear instructions and practice examples were given for each sub test.

The test was standardised on a sample of 10,132, which consists of both boys and girls. Adequate care had been taken by the test constructor to make the sample a true representative of population. The sample consists of students from VIII, IX, X and XI with their age group ranging from 12 years to 18 + years.

Scoring

A set of scoring stencils has been provided along with the manual. Scoring can be done by putting the relevant stencil key on each page of the answer sheet. A ready reckoner has been provided by the test constructor to convert the test scores into deviation IQ's.

The reliability and validity of the test were obtained by using different methods and were confirmed by each other. Reliability coefficient of the test has been determined by test-retest method and split half method. The reliability coefficient by the test-retest method was found to be 0.84±0.021 and the coefficient of correlation between scores on odd and even items was found to be 0.951±0.004. The reliability coefficient of the whole test using Spearman Brown prophecy formula was found to be 0.974±0.003 which is a very high correlation and hence a very dependable relationship.

Besides being highly reliable, the test is valid too. The validity coefficients of the test have been found out by correlating the percentage of total marks obtained in all the subjects with the total score obtained on the present test. The coefficient of correlation was found to be 0.57±0.043.

The degrees of reliability and validity coefficients were found to be fairly high. Hence, it is concluded that the present test is reliable and valid. (2:1-36).

Ahuja's group test of intelligence was used by Mary Suvarna (1997) in her study "The effectiveness of training in study skills for high school underachievers in relation to their scholastic achievement".

Construction of an Achievement Test in Biology (First Year Pre-university Course)

Though the Pupils' achievement scores in Biology are readily available from school records, they cannot be taken as reliable indices of the achievement because of various reasons such as:

(i) Lack of uniformity in coverage and weightage to content and objectives in their examination/ test papers.

(ii) The defects in evaluation procedure and scoring.

(iii) No standardized test is available to measure the achievement in Biology at the first year P.U.C. Stage.

The following stages and steps were followed in constructing the test.

Stage-I

Step 1: Planning the test—Preparation of blue print in respect of new syllabus.

Step 2: Preparing the test—Pooling and writing of items.

Stage II

Step 3: Trying out the test

Step 4: Item Analysis in terms of – (i) Difficulty Index and (ii) Item validity

Stage III

Step 5: Finalization of items based on item analysis.

Stage IV

Step 6: Evaluation of the test in terms of (i) Reliability, and (ii) Validity

The above mentioned steps are described in detail in the following pages.

Step 1: Planning the test

Very careful planning is required for the preparation of an achievement test. The first and the foremost step in planning a test is to define the objectives that are to be measured by the test. If the objectives and outcomes are clear cut and readily identified, the problem would be comparatively simple.

The objectives of Biology instruction may be of various categories such as factual information, understanding, application, skills etc. The learning outcomes can be evaluated through an essay type as well as objective type questions. But the investigator has chosen objective type questions specially the multiple choice type of questions for the test, because of its objectivity. The objective type questions were of multiple choice type as such questions assess better knowledge, understanding, application and skill type of learning outcome.

Construction of an achievement test is depending more and more on curricular validity. Outline of content is important because the content is the actual vehicle through which the objectives are to be achieved. So the test should reflect all or approximate portion of different topics of the syllabus. Particularly, the present test was prepared covering all the syllabus prescribed for first year P.U.C.

Biology by the Pre-University Board, Karnataka. The researcher has consulted the Common Entrance Test papers of 1994 and 1995, annual examination question papers of various colleges and question banks based on new syllabus. Care has been taken to see that the items present an adequate sampling of the entire unit and the worth of effectiveness of each item depends not only upon its desirability for inclusion in the curriculum and upon its difficulty but also upon its power to discriminate between pupils of high and low levels of general achievement.

Preparing the Test Blue Print

After specifying the content, the objectives and forms of the questions the blue print was prepared in order to give adequate weightage to objectives and the sub-units of the content. Content outline and statement of type of objectives represent the two dimensions into which the test plan should be fitted. These two dimensions need to be put together to give a complete framework and to see which objectives relate specifically to which segment of the content.

A two dimensional chart showing coverage of content and objectives was prepared by referring the First P.U.C. text book of Biology. In consultation with experts in methodology and evaluation, guiding professor, lecturers in Biology and with personal experience in teaching Biology weightages for objectives and content were assigned.

Step 2: Preparing the Test—pooling and Writing of Items

After preparing the design of the test, items were pooled and written by referring to textbooks, reference books, question papers and question banks prepared by Department of Pre-University Education. Multiple choice type of items were prepared as they are regarded as the most valuable and most generally applicable of the test forms. Test consists of 90 items and out of these, sixty-six items are collected from different sources and twenty four items are prepared by the researcher. Out of them, eighty items are multiple choice items and ten items are drawing items to test their skill. The items thus prepared were

Table 3.3: Blue Print for Achievement Test in Biology (I-PUC)

Objectives Content	*Knowledge*	*Understanding*	*Application*	*Skill*	*Total*
1 Botany (36 hrs)					
Unit 1:					
Diversity of plant life on Earth (2 hrs)	1(1)	1(1)	1(1)	-	3(3)
Unit 2:					
Kigdom Monera (4 hrs)	1(1)	1(1)	2(2)	2(1)	6(5)
Unit 3:					
Kingdom Protista Kingdom Mycota (3 hrs)	1(1)	1(1)	2(2)	-	4(4)
Unit 4:					
Kingdom Metaphyta or Plantae (22 hrs)	7(7)	9(9)	8(8)	6(3)	30(27)
Unit 5:					
Taxonomy of Angiosperms (5 hrs)	2(2)	2(2)	1(1)	2(1)	7(6)
Sub Total	12 (12)	14(14)	14(14)	10(5)	50(45)

(Contd...)

Table 3.3: Contd...

Objectives Content	*Knowledge*	*Understanding*	*Application*	*Skill*	*Total*
II Zoology (36 hrs)					
Unit 1:					
Introduction to Biology (4hrs)	2(2)	2(2)	2(2)	-	6(6)
Unit 2:					
Diversity of Animal life (14hrs)	5(5)	6(6)	5(5)	2(1)	18(17)
Unit 3:					
Type study (5hrs)	1(1)	3(3)	1(1)	2(1)	7(6)
Unit 4:					
Unity of life (8hrs)	3(3)	1(1)	4(4)	4(2)	12(10)
Unit 5:					
Cell division (5 hrs)	1(1)	2(2)	2(2)	2(1)	7(6)
Sub Total	12(12)	14(14)	14(14)	10(5)	50(45)
Grand Total	24(24)	28 (28)	28 (28)	20 (10)	100 (90)

Note: The numbers outside the bracket indicate the marks.
The numbers inside the bracket indicate the number of items.
The hours in the content column indicate the teaching hours prescribed by the Department of Pre-University Education.

scrutinised by evaluation experts and senior lecturers in Biology from Pre-University colleges. In the light of the suggestions given by them, necessary modifications were made in certain items. Thus a draft consists of 90 items for the tryout. Specific directions for administration of the test mentioning time limit, preliminary test was prepared for 100 marks. Questionnaire was developed in consultation with specialists and in accordance with the conventional procedures set for test construction. See Appendix-B for the Draft Achievement test in Biology with the directions and scoring key.

Step 3: Trying out the Test

After the test was prepared according to plan it was ready to be given a trial in actual use. The questionnaire was scrutinised to correct the typographical errors if any. Since, it is impossible in advance to know exactly how good the test is or to locate the weaker items, the try out should be considered as one of the important necessary steps in constructing the final form. (25:82).

The purpose of the experimental tryout is to obtain data concerning the following:

1. The difficulty of each test item.
2. The discriminating power of each test item.
3. The effectiveness of each distracter for each multiple choice test item.
4. The adequacy of the directions, the time limits and the test format. (15:285)

The final draft thus prepared was tried out on a sample of 296 students attending first year Pre-university in various pre-university colleges of Chitradurga district, which were selected at random. The time taken by the students to answer the test ranged from one hour twenty minutes to one hour forty minutes.

Step 4: Item Analysis

The test was administered to 296 pupils and their answer books were scored and master chart containing question wise marks and total marks was prepared. For the purpose of determining item difficulty indices and item validity, the scores were arranged in descending order. The answer papers were divided into 3 groups such as high group, average group and low group. The upper 27 per cent of the answer papers forms high group and the lower 27 per cent of the answer papers forms the lower group and the rest 46 per cent were taken as the average group.

The number of answer papers in both the extreme groups came to 80 as the total number of papers were 296. The average group was kept aside and paper of the other two groups (High and Low groups) were taken for item analysis.

Index of Difficulty

The difficulty index is defined as the percentage of the group who answered the item correctly. The larger the value of the index is, the easier the item.

The numerical value of the index of difficulty of a test item is nor determined solely by the content of the item. It reflects also the ability of the group responding to the item. (9: 228).

Difficulty index was calculated using the following formula:

$$DI = PH + PL/2$$

Where,

DI = Index of item difficulty

PH = Percentage of high group value, and

PL = Percentage of low group value.

The table indicating item difficulty indices is given below:

Table 3.4: Difficulty Indices of 90 Items of Achievement Test in Biology (n = 296)

Item number	*Percentage of Higher Group Value (PH) (No. of persons answered correctly in higher group)*	*Percentage of Lower Group Value (PL) (No. of persons answered correctly in lower group)*	*DI = (PH + PL) /2*
1	80	53	67
2	65	23	44
3	99	60	80
4	93	31	62
5	84	43	64
6	69	33	51
7	90	45	68
8	88	26	57
9	45	38	42
10	86	54	70
11	98	40	69
12	95	64	80
13	55	30	43
14	93	40	67
15	24	24	24
16	53	55	54
17	44	10	27
18	86	56	71
19	13	31	22
20	10	28	19
21	96	49	73
22	74	31	53
23	51	25	38
24	66	23	45
25	80	43	62
26	65	30	48

Item Number	*PH*	*PL*	*DI = (PH + PL) /2*
27	38	16	27
28	84	41	63
29	64	20	42
30	95	38	67
31	45	33	39
32	78	38	58
33	35	25	30
34	70	41	56
35	40	30	35
36	53	24	39
37	53	28	41
38	68	35	52
39	54	34	44
40	48	13	31
41	78	24	51
42	99	55	77
43	86	31	59
44	88	28	58
45	23	01	12
46	86	66	76
47	83	39	61
48	100	76	88
49	98	64	81
50	63	11	37
51	83	49	66
52	58	28	43
53	89	55	72
54	88	50	69
55	89	31	60
56	83	28	56
57	84	25	55
58	88	24	56
59	60	36	48

Item Number	PH	PL	DI = (PH + PL) /2
60	53	20	37
61	80	43	62
62	66	23	45
63	95	45	70
64	85	41	63
65	55	16	36
66	93	65	79
67	98	51	75
68	40	19	30
69	69	28	49
70	34	28	31
71	93	25	59
72	60	26	43
73	86	23	55
74	35	10	23
75	93	30	62
76	84	34	59
77	75	34	55
78	49	21	35
79	80	19	50
80	91	23	57
81	44	24	34
82	51	16	34
83	83	50	67
84	55	23	39
85	63	34	49
86	84	31	58
87	94	46	70
88	04	00	02
89	96	60	78
90	84	33	59

Item Validity

The validity index of an item (i.e., its discriminative power) is determined to the extent to which the given item discriminates among examinees who differ sharply in the function (or functions) measured by the test as a whole. A number of methods have been devised for use in determining the discriminative power of an item. But biserial correlation is usually regarded as the standard procedure in item analysis. Biserial' gives the correlation of an item with total score on the test, or with scores in some independent criterion. The adequacy of other methods is judged by the degree to which they are able to yield results which approximate those obtained by biserial correlation (11:365).

In order to determine item validities of short answer type questions and Objective type questions, biserial and point biserial coefficients are calculated by using the corresponding ABACS. (16:414-464).

The biserial and the point biserial coefficients are used as discrimination indices in item analysis. The biserial correlation coefficient describes the relationship between two variables. Score on a test item and score on the total test for each examinee. High positive correlations are obtained for items that high scoring students on the test tend to get right (Item score = +1) and low scoring students on the test tend to get wrong (Item score = 0). Such items are interpreted to be high in discrimination. Negatively discriminating items show the opposite relationship. Most students with high-test scores have scores of zero on the test item and many with low test scores have scores of +1 on the item. The point biserial correlation coefficient differs from the biserial coefficient computationally and theoretically, but for item analysis purposes the two can be interpreted in essentially the same manner. Point biserial correlation coefficient is calculated for objective type items and biserial correlation coefficients for short answer type items (Drawing items).

Table 3.5: Validities of Items of Achievement Test in Biology (n=296)

Item No.	*Percentage of pupils passed in the higher group (% PH)*	*Percentage of pupils passed in the lower group (% PL)*	r_b/r_{pb}	*Value*
1	80	53	r_{pb}	0.35
2	65	23	r_{pb}	0.50
3	99	60	r_{pb}	0.61
4	93	31	r_{pb}	0.68
5	84	43	r_{pb}	0.51
6	69	33	r_{pb}	0.43
7	90	45	r_{pb}	0.57
8	88	26	r_{pb}	0.66
9	45	38	r_{pb}	0.10
10	86	54	r_{pb}	0.42
11	98	40	r_{pb}	0.70
12	95	64	r_{pb}	0.49
13	55	30	r_{pb}	0.31
14	93	40	r_{pb}	0.63
15	24	24	r_{pb}	0.00
16	53	55	r_{pb}	0.08
17	44	10	r_{pb}	0.47
18	86	56	r_{pb}	0.41
19	13	31	r_{pb}	0.28
20	10	28	r_{pb}	0.30
21	96	49	r_{pb}	0.62
22	74	31	r_{pb}	0.51
23	51	25	r_{pb}	0.33
24	66	23	r_{pb}	0.51
25	80	43	r_{pb}	0.46
26	65	30	r_{pb}	0.42
27	38	16	r_{pb}	0.31
28	84	41	r_{pb}	0.52

Item No.	*Percentage of pupils passed in the higher group (% PH)*	*Percentage of pupils passed in the lower group (% PL)*	r_b/r_{pb}	*Value*
29	64	20	r_{pb}	0.52
30	95	38	r_{pb}	0.67
31	45	33	r_{pb}	0.15
32	78	38	r_{pb}	0.48
33	35	25	r_{pb}	0.14
34	70	31	r_{pb}	0.36
35	40	30	r_{pb}	0.13
36	53	24	r_{pb}	0.38
37	53	28	r_{pb}	0.32
38	68	35	r_{pb}	0.40
39	54	34	r_{pb}	0.26
40	48	13	r_{pb}	0.48
41	78	24	r_b	0.54
42	99	73	r_b	0.60
43	86	31	r_b	0.58
44	98	28	r_b	0.62
45	23	01	r_b	0.52
46	86	66	r_{pb}	0.29
47	83	39	r_{pb}	0.53
48	100	76	r_{pb}	0.48
49	98	64	r_{pb}	0.55
50	63	11	r_{pb}	0.61
51	83	49	r_{pb}	0.44
52	58	28	r_{pb}	0.38
53	89	55	r_{pb}	0.47
54	88	50	r_{pb}	0.50
55	89	31	r_{pb}	0.64
56	83	28	r_{pb}	0.61
57	84	25	r_{pb}	0.64
58	88	24	r_{pb}	0.68
59	60	36	r_{pb}	0.29

Item No.	*Percentage of pupils passed in the higher group (% PH)*	*Percentage of pupils passed in the lower group (% PL)*	r_b/r_{pb}	*Value*
60	53	20	r_{pb}	0.42
61	80	43	r_{pb}	0.46
62	66	23	r_{pb}	0.51
63	95	45	r_{pb}	0.63
64	85	41	r_{pb}	0.53
65	55	16	r_{pb}	0.49
66	93	74	r_{pb}	0.32
67	98	51	r_{pb}	0.64
68	40	19	r_{pb}	0.29
69	69	28	r_{pb}	0.49
70	34	28	r_{pb}	0.09
71	93	25	r_{pb}	0.71
72	60	26	r_{pb}	0.41
73	86	23	r_{pb}	0.67
74	35	10	r_{pb}	0.38
75	93	30	r_{pb}	0.69
76	84	34	r_{pb}	0.58
77	75	34	r_{pb}	0.49
78	49	21	r_{pb}	0.37
79	80	19	r_{pb}	0.66
80	81	23	r_{pb}	0.71
81	44	24	r_{pb}	0.28
82	51	16	r_{pb}	0.46
83	83	50	r_{pb}	0.42
84	55	23	r_{pb}	0.40
85	63	34	r_b	0.36
86	84	31	r_b	0.54
87	94	46	r_b	0.59
88	04	00	r_b	0.20
89	96	60	r_b	0.60
90	84	33	r_b	0.53

Where r_b = biserial coefficient for short answer items

r_{pb} = Point biserial coefficient for objective type items

Step 5: Finalisation of Items Based on Item Analysis

Index of item difficulty and item validity coefficients are calculated for individual test items. As a result of these two analysis, items numbered 9, 15, 16, 19, 20, 31, 33, 35, 45, 48, 49, 70, 74 and 88 were deleted. The remaining 76 items carrying total of 84 marks constituted the final test. It may be added here that too easy and too difficult items and items giving rise to coefficient less than 0.25 were deleted. (35:245). The test items were arranged on the basis of difficulty level in the final test.

Step 6: Evaluation of Achievement Test in Biology

The final test was evaluated with the help of reliability and validity of thc test.

Reliability of the Test

The reliability of a test is its ability to yield consistent result from one set of measures to another. It refers from one set of measures to another. It refers to the extent to which a measuring device yields consistent result upon testing and retesting. (25:95). The test-retest reliability of the test was worked out (with a test–retest interval of 3 weeks) by administering the test on a representative sample of 130 subjects. The obtained coefficient of test-retest reliability is 0.89.

Consistency reliability was calculated by split half method and it was found to be 0.93 (n=230).

Validity of the Test

A test is a valid one if it measures what it intends to measure or that it must measure the objective or such an aspect of objective as the test claims that it is measuring. It always refers to the purpose of the test. (25:101).

Table 3.6: Weightages in the Final Test

Objectives / *Content (units)*	*Knowledge*	*Understanding*	*Application*	*Skill*	*Total*
Botany					
Unit 1: Diversity of plant life on earth	1(1)	1(1)	1(1)	-	3(3)
Unit 2: Kingdom: Monera	1(1)	1(1)	2(2)	2(1)	6(5)
Unit 3: Kingdom: Protista	1(1)	-	1(1)	-	2(2)
Unit 4: Kingdom: Metaphyta (Plantae)	6(6)	7(7)	6(6)	6(3)	25(22)
Unit 5: Taxonomy of Angiosperms	2(2)	2(2)	-	-	4(4)
Sub Total	11(11)	11(11)	10(10)	8(4)	40(36)

Table 3.6: Contd...

Objectives / *C3ontent (units)*	*Knowledge*	*Understanding*	*Application*	*Skill*	*Total*
Zoology					
Unit 1: Introduction to Biology	2(2)	2(2)	2(2)	-	6(6)
Unit 2: Diversity of Animal Life	4(4)	5(5)	4(4)	2(1)	15(4)
Unit 3: Type study	1(1)	3(3)	1(1)	2(1)	7(6)
Unit 4: Unit of life	2(2)	1(1)	4(4)	2(1)	9(8)
Unit 5: Cell division	1(1)	2(2)	2(2)	2(1)	7(6)
Sub Total	10(10)	13(13)	13(13)	8(4)	44(40)
Grand Total	21(21)	24(24)	23(23)	16(8)	84(76)

Note: The numbers outside the bracket indicate the marks.

The numbers inside the bracket indicate the number of items.

The content validity of the test was examined in terms of coverage of content and instructional objectives.

From the table 3.6 it is evident that the test has content validity as it covers all the units and objectives adequately. Further the test was given to 6 senior lecturers in Biology teaching first year P.U.C. According to their opinion also, the test has content validity.

The concurrent validity of the achievement test in Biology was estimated against the marks obtained in the annual examination of first year P.U.C. (in Biology paper). Raw scores of the annual examination were converted into T-scores. Validity coefficient of 0.75 was obtained (n=130). Intrinsic validities of the test ranged from 0.94 (n=130) to 0.96 (n=230).

The reliability and validity coefficients indicate that the test is a reasonably dependable measure of achievement in Biology for first year pre-university students of Chitradurga district.

Selection of Tools for Assessing Hypethesized Casual Factors

The following tools were administered to over, normal and underachievers to know the effect of the factors on underachievement. The following tools were selected based on review of related literature and personal experience of the investigator.

Science Attitude Scale

Science Attitude Scale was developed by Avinash Grewal (1990). The purpose of this scale would be to know whether or not the students have developed favourable attitudes towards science as a discipline. The underlying assumption being that one of the outcomes of science education is the development of positive attitude towards the subject.

The science attitude has been operationally defined as a generalized attitude towards the universe of science content and being measured in terms of its favourableness or unfavourableness estimated from the scores obtained by the subjects on a attitude scale toward science comprising the four categories from the universe of content "Science Attitude". (1) Positive intellectual (2) Negative intellectual (3) Positive emotional, and (4) Negative emotional attitudes.

Likert method and scale discrimination techniques were used in the construction of Science Attitude Scale.

The Science Attitude Scale is a self-reporting inventory consisting of 20 items designed to assess the attitude of individuals towards science. Out of which ten items are positive and the other ten items are negative. The scale was standardized on a representative sample of 515 higher secondary students of Bhopal. Items were assigned with five point scale such as strongly agree, agree, undecided, disagree and strongly disagree.

Scoring

Each of the ten positive items (Sl. Nos. 2, 4, 6, 8, 10, 12, 14, 16, 18, 20) of the scale was assigned a weight ranging from 4 (strongly agree) to zero (strongly disagree). In case of the ten negative items (Sl. Nos. 1, 3, 5, 7, 9, 11, 13, 15, 17, 19) the scale rating is reversed ranging from zero (strongly agree) to four (strongly disagree). The attitude score of a subject is the sum total of scores on all the twenty items of the scale. For each student a total score on the scale can be obtained by summating his scores for the individual items. Thus a maximum of 80 scores can be obtained by a subject. However the administration of the test reveals that the score is 25-70.

The scale is highly reliable and valid. The reliability of the Science Attitude Scale (SAS) was estimated by the Spilt-Half (0.86) and Test-Retest (0.75) methods which was found to be quite satisfactory. This compares favourably with reliability (0.765) found by Sood (1975) for his scale of

students who should improve their study habits. They can help these students in the optimum use of their valuable time and energy.

(iii) Parents can also use this inventory to guide their children.

The inventory is a self-reporting one. It consists of 45 statements. Against each statement, three modes of responses are provided namely 'A' for 'always or mostly', 'B' for 'sometimes' and 'C' for 'rarely or never'. The student has to respond to each of the statements by ticking (√) mark to one of the responses which describes his/her study habits most appropriately.

Table 3.7: Areas of Study Habits Inventory and the Number of Items Measuring Each Component

Areas	*Number of items*	*Total Number of Items*
1. Budgeting time	1, 2, 3, 4, 32	5
2. Physical Condition	5, 6, 7, 8, 9, 43	6
3. Reading ability	10, 13, 14, 15, 16, 17, 22, 28	8
4. Note taking	11, 18, 19	3
5. Learning Motivation	20, 21, 23, 24, 25, 40	6
6. Memory	12, 26, 27, 37	4
7. Taking examination	29, 30, 31, 33, 34, 35, 36, 38, 39, 42	10
8. Health	41, 44, 45	3
Grand Total		45

Although there is no time limit, the subjects can complete the entire inventory within 20-25 minutes.

Scoring

The procedure of scoring is quite simple. For 'Always' or 'Mostly' response, score of 2 is awarded, where as 1 and 0 scores are to be given for 'Sometimes' or 'Never' responses respectively. In case of statements numbered 6, 9, 13, 15, 24, 26, 34, 36, 37, 41, and 42 the weightage of scoring is reversed and it is 0, 1 and 2 for 'always', 'sometimes' and 'never' responses respectively. The maximum obtainable score is 90. Higher score indicates good study habits.

The inventory is highly reliable and valid. The reliability of the inventory has been determined by two methods.

(i) The reliability coefficient was found to be 0.88 by test-retest method (with an interval of 4 weeks) on a sample of 200 male students of undergraduate classes.

(ii) The reliability coefficient was found to be 0.67 with an interval of 3 months on a sample of 60 girls studying in intermediate classes.

(iii) Using Split-Half techniques on 150 boys of intermediate and undergraduate classes, the coefficient of correlation was found to be 0.56 between odd and even items.

Validity

The inventory, besides having a high face validity has the other coefficients.

The validity coefficients indicate that the inventory has sufficiently high validity with other similar inventories and called measures by other authors and have significant relationship with other variables, which influence the study habits and academic performances. For research purposes, the inventory can safely be recommended for use with the sample for which it has been prepared. (27:1-8).

This tool was used by Deshpande (1984) and Mary Suvarna (1997) in their studies.

Adjustment Inventory for College Students (AICS)

The adjustment inventory was developed by Sinha and Singh (1980). The present inventory has been designed for

Table 3.8: Validity Coefficients of the Study Habits Inventory with Similar Type of Study Habit Inventories

Name of other tests	*N*	*Validity coefficient*
1. Study Habit Inventory —Mukhopadhaya and Sansanwal	80	0.69
2. Test of study habits and Attitudes —C.P. Mathur	80	0.67
3. Study Habit Inventory —B.V. Patel	80	0.74
4. Study Involvement Inventory —Asha Bhatnagar	80	0.83

Table 4.9: Validity Coefficients of the Study Habit Inventory with Other Variable Measures

Name of other Tests	*N*	*Validity Coefficient*
1. Verbal Achievement Motivation Test —V.P. Bhargava	50	0.46
2. Scholastic Achievement (total marks in annual examination)	50	0.42
3. Level of Aspiration —Shah and Bhargava	50	0.58
4. Projective test of Achievement Motivation —P. Deo	50	0.53
5. Reading Comprehension Test —Ahuja and Ahuja	50	0.76

use with college students of India. The test seeks to segregate normal from poorly adjusted students of all grades in respect of five areas of adjustment (home, health, social, emotional and educational).

The inventory has been prepared in Hindi as well in English and it has 102 items (home 16, health 15, social 19, emotional 31 and educational 21). While constructing items, care was taken to formulate items keeping in view the local conditions and the problems facing the students population in this country. It is a self-reporting inventory and there is no time limit for answering it. Ordinarily an individual takes 18 minutes in completing the test. The inventory consists of 102 questions relating to their personality and a separate answer sheet is provided to the subjects to mark their responses as 'Yes' or 'No'.

The final test of 102 items was administered on a randomly selected representative sample of 2280 students (1550 males and 730 females). The chi-square test was applied to determine the normality of the distributions of the scores of the subjects of the two sexes in respect of the total inventory as also the five separate areas of the inventory. The values of chi-square thus calculated, showed that the distributions were not departing significantly from normality.

Scoring

Transparent scoring keys are provided for each area and the responses marked under circle is considered and each has assigned a weightage of one score. Low scores indicate satisfactory adjustment and high scores indicate unsatisfactory adjustment.

The test is highly reliable and it is evident from the reliability coefficients. The coefficients of reliability was determined by (i) split half method (ii) K.R. formula 20 (iii) Hoyt's analysis of variance method. Test-retest was also determined by administering the test after a period of 3 weeks of 228 students which is 10 per cent of the total sample. The following table gives the reliability coefficients determined by different methods.

Besides being highly reliable, the test is valid too. In item analysis validity coefficients were determined for each

Table 3.10: Reliability Coefficients of the Adjustment Inventory by Using Different Methods

Method used	*Home (a)*	*Health (b)*	*Social (c)*	*Emotional (d)*	*Educational (e)*	*Total*
Split half	0.87	0.83	0.96	0.95	0.97	0.94
Test-retest	0.85	0.82	0.95	0.94	0.96	0.93
Hoyt's method	0.86	0.85	0.95	0.95	0.940	0.94
K.R. Formula 20	0.84	0.82	0.92	0.94	0.93	0.92

item by biserial correlation method and only such items were retained which yielded biserial correlation with both the criteria (i) total score and (ii) area score, significant at .001 level. Inter-correlations among the five areas of the inventory were calculated.

Table 3.11: Correlation Matrix of the Five Areas of Adjustment Inventory

Areas	*A*	*B*	*C*	*D*	*E*
(a) Home	-	0.22	0.16	0.26	0.25
(b) Health	0.22	-	0.14	0.25	0.22
(c) Social	0.16	0.14	-	0.21	0.20
(d) Emotional	0.26	0.25	0.21	-	0.32
(e) Educational	0.25	0.22	0.20	0.32	-

The above table reveals that correlations among various areas vary from 0.14 to 0.32 with an average of 0.22. Thurston's centroid method of factor analysis was employed and after the extractions of second centroid factor from the first residual correlation matrix, it was amply proved that there exists inter-dependence among the five areas of inventory.

The inventory was also validated by correlating inventory scores with Hostel Superintendents ratings. Product moment coefficient of correlation between the inventory scores and superintendents ratings was obtained to be 0.58. (32:2-8).

Adjustment inventory for college students was used by Agarwal (1982), Mehta (1987) and Vashishtha (1991) in their studies.

Sinha's Comprehensive Anxiety Test (SCAT)

Comprehensive Anxiety Test was developed by Sinha & Sinha (1990). The items of the test were largely constructed on the basis of the symptoms of anxiety reported by those who visited the Institute of Psychological Research and Service, Patna University for psychological assistance.

The test consists 90 questions and are related to personality of the subjects. Against each question 'Yes' or 'No' responses have been printed. Their task is to encircle one of those two responses which they think has a relation to their personality. There is no right or wrong answer. They are designed to study individual reactions to different situations. They have to encircle 'Yes' when the content of the question is correct as far as their personality is concerned. The 'No' response is encircled when they do not agree with the question. No time limit is fixed for completing the test. However, usually an individual takes 15 to 20 minutes in completing the test form.

Scoring

The inventory can be scored accurately by hand and no scoring key or stencil is provided. For any response indicated as 'Yes', the testee should be awarded the score of one, and zero for 'No'. The sum of all the positive or yes responses would be the total anxiety score of the individual.

The test is highly reliable and valid. The coefficient of reliability was determined by using the two methods.

(i) The test-retest method (N=100) was employed to determine the temporal stability of the test.

The product moment correlation between the test and retest scores was 0.85.

(ii) The internal consistency reliability was ascertained by adopting odd-even procedure (N=100). Using the Spearman Brown formula, the reliability coefficient of the test was found to be 0.92.

Both the values ensure a high reliability of the test.

The coefficient of validity was determined by computing the coefficient of correlation between scores on Comprehensive Anxiety Test and on Taylor's Manifest Scale. It was 0.62, which is significant beyond 0.001 level of confidence (33:3-7).

This test was used by Chaudhari Jain (1975) Sushila Tandon (1977), Tripathi (1978), Homchaudhari (1980) and Srivastava (1985) in their studies on correlates of achievement.

Self-Concept Questionnaire (SCQ)

Self concept questionnaire was developed by Rajkumar Saraswat. Saraswat and Gaur (1981) described self concept – "The self concept is the individual's way of looking at himself. It also signifies his way of thinking, feeling and behaving".

The self concept inventory provides six separate dimensions of self concept i.e., physical, social, intellectual, moral, educational and temperamental self concept. It also gives a total self concept score. The operational definitions of self concept dimensions measured by this inventory are:

1. *Physical:* Individual's view of their body, health, physical appearance and strength.
2. *Social:* Individual's sense of worth in social interactions.
3. *Temperamental:* Individual's view of their prevailing emotional state or predominance of a particular kind of emotional reaction.

4. *Educational:* Individual's view of themselves in relation to school, teachers and extracurricular activities.
5. *Moral:* Individual's estimation of their moral worth; right and wrong activities.
6. *Intellectual:* Individual's awareness of their intelligence and capacity of problem solving and judgements.

Table 3.12: Self-Concept Dimensions along with Their Item Numbers

Self-concept dimensions	*Code No.*	*Item Numbers*
Physical	A	2, 3, 9, 20, 22, 27, 29, 31
Social	B	1, 8, 21, 37, 40, 43, 46, 48
Temperamental	C	4, 10, 14, 16, 19, 23, 24, 28
Educational	D	5, 13, 15, 17, 25, 26, 30, 32
Moral	E	6, 34, 35, 41, 42, 44, 45, 47
Intellectual	F	7, 11, 12, 18, 33, 36, 38, 39

The inventory contains 48 items. Each dimension contains 8 items. Each item is provided with five alternatives. Responses are obtained on the test booklet itself. There is no time limit but generally 20 minutes have been found sufficient for responding all the items.

The self-concept questionnaire was standardized on 1000 students of 20 higher secondary schools of Delhi, with the age group ranging from 14 to 18 years of both the sexes.

Scoring

The respondent is provided with five alternatives to give his responses ranging from most acceptable to least acceptable descriptions of his self-concept. The alternatives or responses are arranged in such a way that the scoring system for all the items will remain the same that is, 5, 4, 3, 2, 1 whether items are positive or negative. If the respondent put (√) mark for first alternative the score is 5, for second alternative the score is 4, for third alternative the score is 3, for the fourth it is 2 and for the fifth and last alternative the score is one. The summated score of all the 48 items provide the total self-concept score of an individual. A high score on this inventory indicates a higher self-concept, while a low score shows low self-concept.

The test is highly reliable and valid. The reliability of the inventory was found by test-retest method and it was found to be 0.91 for the total self-concept measure. Reliability coefficients of its various dimensions varies from 0.67 to 0.88.

Experts' opinion were obtained to establish the validity of the inventory. One hundred items were given to 25 psychologists to classify the items to the category to which it belongs. Items of highest agreement and not less than 80 per cent of agreement were selected. Thus, the content and construct validity were established. (28:3-7).

Kakkar Socio-economic Status Scale (KSESS)

Socio-economic status scale was developed by Kakkar (1993). The test is used to measure the socio-economic status of over, normal and underachievers in Biology among pre-university students of Chitradurga district. Socio-economic status of an individual is a sort of rank or position as determined by the joint influence of his social and economic rankings in the society he belongs to More precisely, it is one's place on the socio-economic scale. Such status emerges in accordance with the degree of his prestige in the social structure and the slab of income he happens to earn.

The present SES scale has been constructed to obtain an individual's social and economic status integrally. It is equally applicable to both urban and rural populations. The scale, though initially developed for undergraduate, graduate and post-graduate students, is equally usable on all kinds of population as SES is a measure that every individual or group, irrespective of educational level, sex, age, caste, creed etc., may be subjected to. It can be administered both individually and to a group.

The scale was prepared with the help of the hierarchies and items as determined by the judges and experts. This form was administered to a randomly chosen sample of 450 students, an analysis of such students in any college of the state had earlier revealed that they came from almost all parts of the state, rural as well as urban, that they were almost an evenly mixed group of different religions, sex, castes and communities and they were typical of the various socio-economic status of the population. Thus the sample was truly representative of the college students in the state.

The form of the scale has been detailed below.

Table 3.13: Areas of Socio-economic Status with their Item Numbers

Sl.No.	*Area*	*Item No.*
1.	Parent's educational standards	1
2.	Professional or occupational position of parents	2
3.	Income standards	3
4.	Living conditions of family	4
5.	Caste	5
6.	Family's landed property	6.7
7.	Family's material possessions	8
8.	Urban/rural locale	Identifying particulars

Monthly income of parents in the Kakkar's SES scale is modified as per the All India Average working class consumer price index.

Income range in the Kakkar's scale	*Modified as*
1. Upto Rs. 400/-	1. Upto Rs. 1300/-
2. Rs. 401 to Rs. 600/-	2. Rs. 1301 to 2000/-

3.	Rs. 601 to 800/-	3.	Rs. 2001 to 2600/-
4.	Rs. 801 to 1000/-	4.	Rs. 2601 to 3300/-
5.	Rs. 1001 to 2000/-	5.	Rs. 3301 to 6500/-
6.	Rs. 2001 to 3000/-	6.	Rs. 6501 to 9700/-
7.	Above Rs. 3000/-	7.	Above Rs. 9700/-

Scoring

Scoring of the scale is simple and objective. Scoring key which provides weightage of each item converts the responses (shown as ticked mark (√) into a quantitative score. The separate scores for each area are then totally vertically to get one's score on SES.

The scale is highly reliable and valid. Reliability of the scale has been calculated by test-retest method. The scale was administered to a sample of 110 randomly chosen students out of the main sample of 450 students and after a two-week interval it was re-administered to the same sample. The correlation between two sets of scores was calculated by Spearman-Brown Prophesy formula. The item wise reliability coefficient ranged from 0.66 to 0.80 and that for scale as a whole came to 0.72. Inter-score reliability coefficients were 0.87 for total Socio-economic status score and from 0.82 to 0.88 for itemwise scores.

The content validity of the scale may be fairly high as the areas and their items are well established by several research studies. Statistical validity index is 0.77. The biserial coefficient of correlation for the total score came to 0.77 which was statistically significant at 0.01 level, and is hence a satisfactory validity index.

There is no time limit to record the responses in the scale, though not more than seven to ten minutes are taken by an individual to complete it.

As the scale constructed is capable of being given and scored in exactly the same manner with every administration, and as its validity, reliability and objectivity stand established, the scale can be said to be standardized. (21:3-11)

Reasons for Selecting the above Mentioned Tools for the Present Study

1. The tools have been prepared on college going students as the sample of the study.
2. The selected tools have high validity and reliability coefficients.
3. The selected tools can be administered to a group of 40-50 students without any difficultly.
4. The inventories/tests can be easily understood by the average students.
5. The system of scoring of the above tests is easy and can be done quickly.
6. The inventories/tests have been specially developed to suit Indian conditions.
7. The above mentioned tools were used by many investigators in their studies.

Sampling

The primary purpose of research is to discover principles that have universal application. But, to study a whole population in order to arrive at a generalisation would be impracticable if not impossible. Given the dynamic nature of population, it is possible that the characteristics of the population would change by the time the research in studying those population are completed. It becomes important to study such population as they exist at the time of research and report them to the relative to a time frame.

After finalising the variables of the present study, consideration was given to whether the entire population is to be made the subject for data collection or a particular group is to be selected as representative of the whole population. The entire population here refers to all the first year pre-university science (Physics, Chemistry, Mathematics and Biology) students of Chitradurga district. Selection of a group as a representative of the entire population was found to be more convenient and suitable. This technique leads to a considerable saving of time, effort and finance. The number of students selected is small, and so it is possible to make a detailed and intensive study. This generally leads to more accurate and reliable results.

The process of sampling makes it possible to draw valid conclusions or generalisations on the basis of careful observation or manipulation of variables within a relatively small proportion of the total universe. Samples are not selected haphazardly but are chosen in a deliberate way so that the influence of chance of probability can be estimated.

The purpose of the present study is to identify the factors causing underachievement in Biology among first year pre-university students of Chitradurga district.

The population from which the sample for the study was drawn, consisted of students studying during the year 1997-98 in first pre-university science classes of both government and private pre-university colleges of Chitradurga district. Data was collected regarding the numbers of pre-university colleges (with science combination) in Chitradurga district (1997-98).

The sample was selected using proportionate stratified random sampling procedure. This procedure was preferred in order to give representation to all types of pre-university colleges and also to make the sample true representative of the population.

At first stage, 10 pre-university colleges were selected. At the second stage the numbers of first pre-university Biology students from each college were selected proportionately. Both at the first and the second stage, the sample has been drawn randomly.

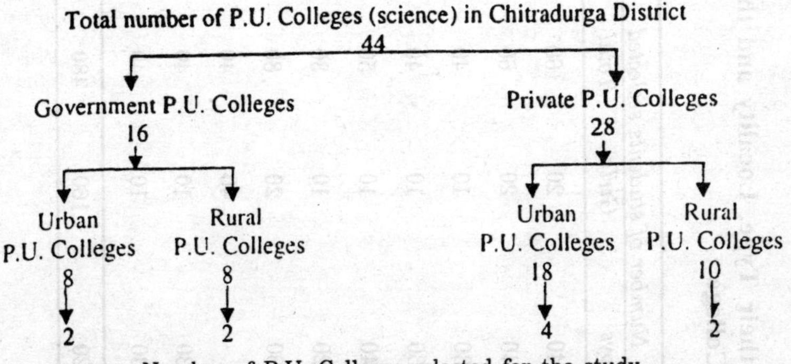

Figure 2: Flow Chart of Sampling

At the first stage, the P.U. colleges have been drawn randomly by using lots in the ratio 5:1 and one more for the fractions there of. At the second stage random numbers have been used to select the required numbers of first pre-university Biology students from each P.U. College.

The details regarding the number of pre-university colleges, the number of boys and girls drawn from each college is presented in the table to follow.

The sample was considered to be fairly true representative of the population since it included all categories of pre-university colleges and the sample included both boys and girls studying in both government and private, urban and rural pre-university colleges of Chitradurga district. The proportion of the sample of urban and rural pre-university students is in the ratio of 2:1 (320:160), boys and girls sample is also in the ratio of 2:1 (320:160).

Administration and Scoring of the Tests

The researcher administered the following tools to the selected sample in order to obtain the required data. Group test of intelligence, achievement test in Biology, science attitude scale, achievement motive test, study habits

Table 3.14: Statement Showing the Number of Pre-university Colleges—their Type, Locality and the Number of Biology Students Drawn from each Pre-university College

Sl. No	*Name of the pre-university college*	*Locality of the college*	*Type of college Govt./Private*	*Number of students seclected*		
				Boys	*Girls*	*Total*
1.	S.T.J. Pre-University College, Davangere	U	P	40	20	60
2.	D.R. M. Science College, Davangere	U	P	40	20	60
3.	S.J. V. P. College, Harihar	U	P	30	10	40
4.	Ideal P.U. College, Chitradurga	U	P	30	10	40
5.	K.N. Pre-University College, Holalkere	R	P	40	10	50
6.	Nalanda P.U. College, Jagalur	R	P	20	10	30
7.	Mothiveerappa Govt. P.U. College, Davangere	U	G	60	20	80
8.	R.S. Govt. P.U. College, Davangere	U	G	-	40	40
9.	Govt. P.U. College, Hosadurga	R	G	30	10	40
10.	Govt. P.U. College, Hiriyur	R	G	30	10	40
			Total	320	160	480

Note: U = Urban, R = Rural, P = Private College, G = Govt. College inventory, adjustment inventory for college students, comprehensive anxiety test, self-concept questionnaire and SES scale were administered to the selected students on different sessions from the third week of February to the second week of March during the year 1998. The researcher has selected this period for administration of tests because in most of the P.U. Colleges the syllabus of first year class would have been completed by the second week of February and annual examinations would commence in the third week of March. This is done to ensure that all students are at a uniform level of subject attainment. The tools require 4 hrs 15 minutes for the actual administration of the tests, besides the investigator had spent nearly 11/2 hours for establishing rapport, giving instructions, distributing and collecting the booklets etc. the tests were administered in 4 sessions. Group test of intelligence was administered in one session. Achievement test in Biology in another session and the other tests were administered in 2 sessions of 2 hours each.

The administration of the tests were done by the investigator himself. About 2-3 class teachers were present during testing. They helped the investigator to administer the tests efficiently.

The following points were kept in view while administering the tools:

1. The directions for each tool were given exactly as provided in the cover sheet of the booklet.

2. General instructions found on the cover page were clearly read out and explained with given examples.

3. The time factor was controlled by the use of a stop watch.

4. The students were further instructed to turn the pages of the test booklets only when they were told do so.

5. The students were informed well in advance to prepare for the achievement test in Biology.

6. Seating arrangements were made as it was done for examinations. (2 students were seated in each bench).
7. The researcher has taken the help of Biology lecturers while distributing and collecting the booklets and also to maintain discipline in the test hall.

When the testing in ten pre-university colleges was completed, the sample obtained was 480, but some of the students had to be rejected because they were not present for all the tests. Finally a sample of 420 was available for analysis.

Scoring

Scoring was done following the guidelines, scoring stencils and scoring keys provided in the respective test manuals. Scoring key for Achievement test in Biology was developed by the researcher and the same was used in scoring of answer scripts. After careful scoring, the raw scores were obtained in respect of each. The raw scores obtained from the intelligence test were converted into DIQ's with the help of a ready reckoner given by the author in the manual for group test of intelligence.

To make the raw scores obtained from the other tests meaningful, they were subjected to various statistical tools so that the significance of various hypotheses could be tested. In the following pages, the researcher has discussed the various statistical techniques used for the analysis of data.

Statistical Techniques used for Analysis of Data

The researcher has used the following statistical techniques for the analysis of data.

1. (*a*) Coefficient of correlation was calculated to establish validity and reliability of the achievement test in Biology (for the test constructed by the investigator).

   (*b*) Biserial and point biserial coefficients of correlations were calculated (item validity coefficients) to select the items (in the test constructed by the researcher).

(c) Coefficient of correlation was calculated for the obtained achievement scores and DIQ's of the students. This information has been used while developing regression equation.

(d) Coefficient of correlation was calculated between dependent and independent variables.

(e) Intercorrelation between independent variables was also calculated.

2. Regression equation was developed to classify the sample into over, normal and underachievers.
3. Single classification analysis of variance (one way ANOVA) was used to test the hypotheses.
4. Whenever 'F' value was found to be significant, Duncan procedure (Multiple range test) was used to test the significance of the mean difference of only 2 groups.

In summary, this chapter has given a detailed account of the methodology adopted by the researcher in the present study. In the next chapter, the analysis and interpretation of the data has been presented and discussed.

REFERENCES

1. Agarwal, S. "The Study of Causes and their Remedial Measures of Two Groups of X and XII Class of Relatively Identical Intelligence but Differing in Educational Achievements". Gorakhpur University, 1982. In Buch, M.P. (Ed.), *Fourth Survey of Research in Education (1983-1988),* Vol. 1, New Delhi: N.C.E.R.T., 1991.
2. Ahuja, G.C. *Manual for Group Test of Intelligence.* Agra: National Psychological Corporation, 1976, pp. 1-36.
3. BASE. *CET-Correspondence Course, Biology,* Vol. 1 to 10, Bangalore: No.14, Bull Temple Road, Basavanagudi, 1994.

4. Bhargava, V.P. *Revised Manual for Achievement Motive Test.* Agra: National Psychological Corporation, 1994, pp. 2-7.

5. Chauhan, S.S. *Advanced Educational Psychology.* Fourth revised edition, New Delhi: Vikas Publishing House Pvt. Ltd., 1992.

6. Deo, Prathibha and Mohan, Asha, *Manual for Deo-Mohan Achievement Motivation (N-Ach) Scale.* Agra: National Psychological Corporation, 1985.

7. Deshpande, A.S. "A Study of Determinants of Achievement of Students at the SSC Examination in the Pune Division of Maharashtra State". Poona University, 1984. In Buch, M.P. (Ed.), *Fourth Survey of Research in Education (1983-1988).* Vol.-1, New Delhi: N.C.E.R.T., 1991.

8. Ebel, Robert L. *Measuring Educational Achievement.* Prentice-Hall, India.

9. Ebel, Robert L. and Frisbie, David A. *Essentials of Educational Measurement.* Fifth edition, New Delhi: Prentice Hall of India Private Limited, 1991, p.228.

10. Farquhar, W.W. and Payne, D.A. "A Classification and Comparison of Techniques used in Selecting Under and Overachievers". *Personnel and Guidance Journal,* 1964, 42, pp. 674-684.

11. Garret, Henry E. *Statistics in Psychology and Education.* Bombay: Vakils, Feffer and Simons Ltd., 1981, pp. 151-181, 365.

12. Government of India. *Report of the Education Commission (1964-66).* New Delhi: Ministry of Education, 1966.

13. Gowan, J.C. "Dynamics of Underachievement of Gifted Students". *Indian Educational Review,* N.C.E.R.T., 3, 2, July 1968, pp. 153-167.

14. Grewal, Avinash, *Manual for Science Attitude Scale.* Agra: National Psychological Corporation, 1990, pp. 2-8.

15. Gronlund, Norman E. *Measurement and Evaluation in Teaching.* Third edition, New York: Mac Millan Publishing Co., Inc., 1976. p. 285.

16. Guilford, J.P. *Psychometric Methods.* Second edition, New Delhi: Tata Mc Graw Hill Publishing Co. Ltd., 1984, pp. 414-464.

17. Guilford, J.P. *Fundamental Statistics in Psychology and Education.* Fourth edition, New York: Mc Graw Hill Book Company, 1965, p. 368.

18. Hocking, Thomas Kenneth. "A Case Study Approach to the Understanding of Underachieving Students in a Selected High School Setting". The University of Wisconsin. 1965. *Dissertation Abstracts International*, 26, 9, March 1966, p. 5235.

19. John, C.D. *Predictive Correlates of Creativity of IX Standard Students in the City of Bangalore.* Unpublished Doctoral Dissertation. Bangalore University, Bangalore, 1996, pp. 119-122.

20. Johnson, D.W. The Social Psychology of Education, New York: Holt, Rinehart and Winston Inc., 1970. In John, C.D. *Predictive Correlates of Creativity of IX Standard Students in the City of Bangalore.* Unpublished Doctoral Dissertation, Bangalore University, Bangalore, 1996, p.120.

21. Kakkar, S.B. *Manual for Kakkar Socio-economic Status Scale.* Agra: National Psychological Corporation, 1993. pp.3-11.

22. Mary Suvarna. *The Effectiveness of Training in Study Skills for High School Underachievers in Relation to their Scholastic Achievement.* Unpublished Doctoral Dissertation, Kuvempu University, 1997.

23. M.C.C. Publications. *Biology.* Karnataka Entrance Test-1995, Bangalore: No.3, 16th Cross, 3rd Block, Jayanagar, 1995.

24. Mehta, C.P. "An Investigation into the Effect of Some Psychological Factors on School Achievement of SC and ST Students and the States as Identified by the Baxi Commission in Saurastra". Sardar Patel University, 1987. In Buch, M.B. (Ed.), *Fourth Survey of Research in Education (1983-1988),* Vol. 1, New Delhi: N.C.E.R.T., 1991.

25. Mohanty, Susandhya, *Teaching of Science in Secondary Schools.* New Delhi: Deep and Deep Publication, F-159, Rajouri Garden, 1996, pp. 82-101.

26. Nair, P.K.G. et al. *A Test Book of Biology.* Vol. 1, (First year Pre-university), Bombay: Himalaya Publishing House, 1995.

27. Palsane, M.N. and Sadhna Sharma, *Manual for Palsane and Sharma Study Habit Inventory,* Agra: National Psychological Corporation, 1990, pp. 1-8.

28. Saraswat, Rajkumar, *Manual for Self Concept Questionnaire.* Agra: National National Psychological Corporation, 1984, pp. 3-7.

29. Sarin, C. *Objective Evaluation in Biology,* New Delhi: Tata Mc Graw Hill Publishing Company Ltd., 1989.

30. Saxena, P.C. "A Study of Interests, Need Patterns and Adjustment Problems of Over and Underachievers". Allahabad University, 1972. *Indian Dissertation Abstracts,* 17, July-Sept. 1988, pp.258-265.

31. Seetharam, P.L., Thulajappa, Y. and Chavan, R.R. *Text Book of Biology.* Vol. 1., Bangalore: Expert Educational Publishers, 1996.

32. Sinha, A.K.P. and Singh, R.P. *Manual for Adjustment Inventory for College Students.* Agra: National Psychological Corporation, 1980. pp.2-8.

33. Sinha, A.K.P. and Sinha, L.K.P. *Manual for Sinha's Comprehensive Anxiety Test.* Agra: National Psychological Corporation, 1990, pp.3-7.

34. Skinner, Charles E. *Educational Psychology*, Fourth edition, New Delhi: Printice Hall of India Private Limited, 1989, pp. 102, 265.

35. Thorndike, R. *Personnel Selection Test and Measurement Techniques* New York: John Wiley and Sons Inc., February, 1966, p.245.

36. Tolor, Alexander, "Incidence of Underachievement at High School Level". *Journal of Educational Research,* N.C.E.R.T., 63, 2, Oct. 1969, pp.63-64.

37. Tuckman, Bruce W. *Conducting Educational Research.* New York: Harcourt Brace Jovanovich Inc., 1978, pp. 58-59.

38. Vashistha, K.K. "A Comparative Study of the Adjustment of High and Low Achieving Indian Pupils at Higher Secondary Level". *Journal of Educational Research and Extension,* 27, 3, Jan. 1991, pp. 181-191.

4

Analysis and Interpretation of Data

In the previous chapter on methodology of the study, variables, tools used for the collection of data, sampling and the statistical techniques used in the study are discussed.

In this chapter, the data collected are analysed, discussion is done and the results obtained are interpreted.

Relationship of Independent Variables to the Dependent Variable

Table 4.1: Co-efficient of Correlation of Independent Variables and the Dependent Variable

Sl.No.	*Independent variable*	*Coefficient of correlation of independent variables with Biology achievement scores (V2) N = 420*
1.	Attitude towards science: V3	0.1134*
2.	Achievement motivation: V4	0.1444**
3.	Study habits: V5	0.1772**
4.	Adjustment: V6	-0.2858**
5.	Comprehensive Anxiety: V7	-0.2329**
6.	Self concept: V8	0.2472**
7.	Socio-economic: V9	0.4796**

* *Significant at 0.05 level of probability*
** *Significant at 0.01 level of probability*

Table 4.1 presents the correlations between independent variables namely, attitude towards science, achievement motivation, study habits, adjustment, comprehensive anxiety, self concept and socio-economic status with dependent variable namely, achievement in Biology.

It could be seen from the table that:

- Attitude of students towards science is positively and significantly related to achievement in Biology ($P<0.05$).
- The Achievement motivation is positively and significantly related to achievement in Biology ($P<0.01$).
- The study habits is positively and significantly related to achievement in Biology ($P<0.01$).
- There is negative and significant relationship between adjustment problems and achievement in Biology ($P<0.01$).
- The Comprehensive anxiety is negatively and significantly related to achievement in Biology ($P<0.01$).
- The Self concept is positively and significantly related to achievement in Biology ($P<0.01$).
- The socio-economic status is positively and significantly related to achievement in Biology ($P<0.01$).

Inter-correlations among Independent Variables

Table 4.2 presents Intercorrelations among independent variables for the whole group ($N=420$). The table reveals that the correlation among independent variables is significant except attitude towards science and comprehensive anxiety, SES and achievement motivation, SES and study habits and SES and self concept.

Testing of Hypotheses

The hypotheses formulated were tested using the one way analysis of variance and whenever 'F' value was found

Table 4.2: Intercorrelations Among Independent Variables for the whole Group (N=420)

Variables	*V3*	*V4*	*V5*	*V6*	*V7*	*V8*	*V9*
V3	1.0000						
V4	0.1829** P=0.0000	1.0000					
V5	0.3243** P=0.000	0.2891** P=0.000	1.0000				
V6	-0.1976** P=0.0000	-0.2703** P=0.000	-0.3533** P=0.000	1.0000			
V7	-0.0878 (NS) P=0.072	-0.1693** P=0.000	-0.2177* P=0.000	0.4749** P=0.0000	1.0000		
V8	0.1639** P=0.001	0.3737** P=0.000	0.2184** P=0.000	-0.2766** P=0.000	-0.3824** P=0.000	1.0000	
V9	0.1215* P=0.013	-0.0337 (NS) P=0.491	-0.0041 (NS) P=0.933	-0.1993** P=0.000	-0.2142** P=0.000	0.0937 (NS) P=0.055	1.0000

* *Significant at 0.05 level of probability*

** *Significant at 0.01 level of probability*

NS Nonsignificant

to be significant, Duncan procedure (Multiple Range Test) was used to test the significance of the mean difference of only two groups.

The means and standard deviations of the independent variables and the criterion variable in respect of underachievement, normal achievement and overachievement groups and for the whole group are given in table 4.2.

In order to carry out one way analysis of variance and to test the significance of the mean difference of the groups, the data found in table 4.3 has been made use of.

Hypothesis-1

There is no significant difference between underachievers, normal achievers and overachievers in respect of attitude towards science.

Sub Hypotheses

1.1. There is no significant difference in the mean scores of underachievers and normalachievers in respect of attitude towards science.

1.3. There is no significant difference in the mean scores of underachievers and overachievers in respect of attitude towards science.

1.3. There is no significant different in the mean scores of normalachievers and overachievers in respect of attitude towards science.

The one way ANOVA details of the scores of underachievers, normalachievers and overachievers in respect of attitude towards science of first year P.U.C. Biology students of Chitradurga District are given in the following table.

Since the 'F' value was found to be significant, the researcher was interested in knowing where exactly the difference lies. This was done using Duncan procedure. Duncan ranges for the 0.05 level is 2.79 to 2.93.

Table 4.3: Means and Standard Deviation for the Scores of Independent Variables and the Dependent Variable in Respect of Under, Normal and Overachievement Groups and for the Whole Group

Sl.No.	*Variable*	*Whole Group N=420*		*Underachievement Group N=90*		*Normal achievement Group N=259*		*Overachievement Group N=71*	
1.	V3	49.0571	7.0387	49.9778	7.1861	48.3822	7.0686	50.3521	6.5008
2.	V4	19.5714	4.8231	18.0000	4.4292	19.4054	4.8467	22.1690	4.1952
3.	V5	59.7929	8.4428	57.8667	6.8862	59.9151	9.1812	61.7887	6.8430
4.	V6	41.1429	12.3836	43.6556	11.7695	41.9228	12.6271	35.1127	10.3393
5.	V7	32.5024	14.2096	38.3667	12.1030	31.4247	14.2635	29.0000	14.5445
6.	V8	166.7810	15.7331	158.2444	15.9974	167.4479	14.3287	175.1690	15.2596
7.	V9	31.5905	11.2949	29.3111	10.0086	30.9459	11.8288	36.8310	9.1916
8.	V2	35.9452	15.7940	23.7222	7.6585	34.8224	13.5929	55.5352	12.3112

Table 4.4: Summary of One Way ANOVA of Underachievers, Normalachievers and Overachievers in Respect of Attitude Towards Science

Source	*DF*	*Sum of squares*	*Mean squares*	*F ratio*	*Significance level*
Between groups	2	313.3175	156.6588		*
Within groups	417	20445.3110	49.0295	3.1952	
Total	419	20758.6286			

* *Significant beyond the 0.05 level of probability*

The value actually compared with Mean (J) – (Mean (I) is – $4.9512 \times \text{Range} \times \sqrt{[1/N(I) + 11/N(J)]}$

Table 4.5: Comparison of Mean Scores of Under, Normal and Overachievers in Respect of Attitude Towards Science

Mean	*Group*	*Group 2*	*Group 1*	*Group 3*
48.3822	Group 2			
49.9778	Group 1			
50.3521	Group 3	*		

* Denotes pairs of groups significantly different at the 0.050 level

Note: Group 1 = Underachievers, Group 2 = Normalachievers, Group 3 = Overachievers.

The obtained F value 3.1952 was found to be significant beyond 0.05 level of probability, as it is more than the theoretical value of F. Hence, it may be concluded that there is a significant difference between the scores of underachievers, normalachievers and overachievers in respect of Attitude towards science.

Further Duncans procedure was used to test the significance of difference between the means. It was found that the mean scores of overachievers (50.35) in respect of

Attitude towards science is more than the mean scores of normalachievers (48.38) and underachievers (49.97). The significant difference was found only between overachievers and normalachievers. There is no significant difference between the scores of underachievers and normalachievers, underachievers and overachievers. Hence, the first two sub hypotheses were accepted and the third sub hypothesis was rejected.

From this it may be concluded that overachievers possess high attitude towards science than normal achievers.

Hypotheses-2

There is no significant difference between underachievers, normalachievers and overachievers in respect of achievement motivation.

Sub Hypotheses

2.1. There is no significant difference in the mean scores of underachievers and normalachievers in respect of achievement motivation.

2.2. There is no significant difference in the mean scores of underachievers and overachievers in respect of achievement motivation.

2.3. There is no significant difference in the mean scores of normalachievers and overachievers in respect of achievement motivation.

The one way ANOVA details of the scores of underachievers, normalachievers and overachievers in respect of achievement motivation of first year P.U.C. Biology students of Chitradurga District are given in the following table.

Since the 'F' value was found to be significant, the researcher was interested in knowing where exactly the difference lies. This was done using Duncan procedure. The value actually compared with mean (J) – Mean (I) is

$$3.2920 \times \text{Range} \times \sqrt{1/N(I) + 11/N(J)}$$

Table 4.6: Summary of One Way ANOVA of Underachievers, Normalachievers and Overachievers in Respect of Achievement Motivation

Source	*DF*	*Sum of squares*	*Mean squares*	*F Ratio*	*Significance level*
Between groups	2	708.4529	354.2264	16.3428	**
Within groups	417	9038.4043	21.6748		
Total	419	9746.8571			

** Significant beyond the 0.01 level of probability

Table 4.7: Comparison of Mean Scores of Under, Normal and Overachievers in Respect of Achievement Motivation

Mean	*Group*	*Group 1*	*Group 2*	*Group 3*
18.0000	Group 1			
19.4054	Group 2	*		
22.1690	Group 3	*	*	

* Denotes pairs of groups significantly different at the 0.050 level

The obtained F value 16.3428 was found to be significant beyond 0.01 level of probability, as it is more than the theoretical value of F. Hence, it may be concluded that there is a significant difference between the scores of underachievers, normalachievers and overachievers in respect of achievement motivation.

Further it was found that the mean scores of overachievers (22.1690) in respect of achievement motivation is more than the mean scores of normal achievers (19.4054) and underachievers (18.0000). The significant difference in the mean scores was found between underachievers and overachievers, underachievers and normalachievers, and normalachievers and overachievers groups. Hence, all the three sub hypotheses were rejected. From this, it may be concluded that overachievers possess high achievement motivation when compared to normal and underachievers, whereas underachievers have low achievement motivation when compared to normal and overachievers. The normal achievers have high achievement motivation when compared to underachievers. From these findings it may be concluded that low achievement motivation is one of the causes of underachievement in Biology.

The results obtained in this study are corroborated by the results obtained in the studies that were conducted by Srivastava (1967) and Ghuman (1976).

Hypothesis–3

There is no significant difference between underachievers, normalachievers and overachievers in respect of study habits.

Sub Hypotheses

3.1. There is no significant difference in the mean scores of underachievers and normal achievers in respect of study habits.

3.2. There is no significant difference in the mean scores of underachievers and overachievers in respect of study habits.

3.3. There is no significant difference in the mean scores of normalachievers and overachievers in respect of study habits.

The one way ANOVA details of the scores of underachievers, normalachievers and overachievers in respect of study habits of first year P.U.C. Biology students of Chitradurga District are given in the following table.

Since the 'F' value was found to be significant, the researcher was interested in knowing where exactly the difference lies. This was done using Duncan procedure. The value actually compared with Mean (J) – Mean (I) is –

$$5.9218 \times \text{Range} \times \sqrt{[1 / N(I) + 1 / N(J)]}$$

Table 4.8: Summary of One Way ANOVA of Underachievers, Normalachievers and Overachievers in Respect of Study Habits

Source	*DF*	*Sum of squares*	*Mean squares*	*F Ratio*	*Significance level*
Between groups	2	620.6163	310.3082		
Within groups	417	29246.3623	70.1352	4.4244	*
Total	419	29866.9786			

* Significant beyond the 0.05 level of probability

Table 4.9: Comparison of Mean Scores of Under, Normal and Overachievers in Respect of Study Habits

Mean	*Group*	*Group 1*	*Group 2*	*Group 3*
57.8667	Group 1			
59.9151	Group 2	*		
61.7887	Group 3	*		

* Denotes pairs of groups significantly different at the 0.050 level.

The obtained F value 4.4244 was found to be significant beyond 0.05 level of probability, as it is more than the theoretical value of F. Hence, it may be concluded that there is a significant difference between the scores of underachievers, normalachievers and overachievers in respect of study habits.

Further it was found that the mean scores of overachievers (61.7887) is more than the mean scores of normal achievers (59.9151) and underachievers (57.8667). The significant difference in the mean scores was found between underachievers and overachievers, and underachievers and normalachievers groups. There is no significant difference between the scores of normalachievers and overachievers. Hence, the first two sub-hypotheses were rejected and the third sub hypothesis was accepted.

From this it may be concluded that overachievers possess good study habits than underachievers, underachievers possess poor study habits when compared to normal achievers and overachievers. From these findings it may be concluded that poor study habits is one of the causes of underachievement in Biology.

The results obtained in this study are corroborated by the results obtained in the studies that were conducted by Srivastava (1967), Bhaduri (1971), Saxena (1972) and Sharma (1978).

Hypothesis–4

There is no significant difference between underachievers, normalachievers and overachievers in respect of adjustment.

Sub Hypotheses

4.1. There is no significant difference in the mean scores of underachievers and normal achievers in respect of adjustment.

4.2. There is no significant difference in the mean scores of underachievers and overachievers in respect of adjustment.

4.3. There is no significant difference in the mean scores of normalachievers and overachievers in respect of adjustment.

The one way ANOVA details of the scores of underachievers, normalachievers and overachievers in respect of adjustment of first year P.U.C. Biology students of Chitradurga District are given in the following table.

Since the 'F' value was found to be significant, the researcher was interested in knowing where exactly the difference lies. This was done using Duncan procedure. The value actually compared with Mean (J) – Mean (I) is –

$$8.5486 \times \text{Range} \times \sqrt{[1/N(I) + 1/N(J)]}$$

Table 4.10: Summary of One Way ANOVA of Underachievers, Normalachievers and Overachievers in Respect of Adjustment

Source	*DF*	*Sum of squares*	*Mean squares*	*F Ratio*	*Significance level*
Between groups	2	3307.5522	1653.7761.		
Within groups	417	60947.8764	146.1580	11.3150	**
Total	419	64255.4286			

** Significant beyond the 0.01 level of probability.

Table 4.11: Comparison of Mean Scores of Under, Normal and Overachievers in Respect of Adjustment

Mean	*Group*	*Group 1*	*Group 2*	*Group 3*
35.1127	Group 1			
41.9228	Group 2	*		
43.6556	Group 3	*		

* Denotes pairs of groups significantly different at the 0.050 level

The obtained F value 11.3150 was found to be significant beyond 0.01 level of probability as it is more than theoretical value of F. Hence, it may be concluded that there is a significant difference between the scores of underachievers, normalachievers and overachievers in respect of adjustment.

Further it was found that the mean scores of overachievers (35.1127) in respect of adjustment is less than the mean scores of normal achievers (41.9228) and underachievers (43.6556). In this tool, lower scores indicate good adjustment and higher scores indicate poor adjustment. The significant difference in the mean scores was found between underachievers and overachievers, and normalachievers and overachievers groups. There is no significant difference between the scores of underachievers and normalachievers. Hence, the first sub hypothesis was accepted and the other two sub hypotheses were rejected.

From this, it may be concluded that overachievers possess good adjustment when compared to underachievers and normalachievers. Underachievers possess poor adjustment when compared to overachievers. From these findings, it may be concluded that poor adjustment is one of the causes of underachievement in Biology.

The results obtained in this study are corroborated by the results obtained in the study that was conducted by Srivastava (1976).

Hypothesis–5

There is no significant difference between underachievers, normalachievers and overachievers in respect of comprehensive anxiety.

Sub Hypotheses

5.1. There is no significant difference in the mean scores of underachievers and normal achievers in respect of comprehensive anxiety.

5.2 There is no significant difference in the mean scores of underachievers and overachievers in respect of comprehensive anxiety.

5.3 There is no significant difference in the mean scores of normalachievers and overachievers in respect of comprehensive anxiety.

The one way ANOVA details of the scores of underachievers, normalachievers and overachievers in respect of comprehensive anxiety of first year P.U.C. Biology students of Chitradurga district are given in the following table.

Since the 'F' value was found to be significant, the researcher was interested in knowing where exactly the difference lies. This was done using Duncan procedure. The value actually compared with Mean (J) – Mean (I) is – $9.8145 \times \text{Range} \times \sqrt{[1/N(I) + 1/N(J)]}$

Table 4.12: Summary of One Way ANOVA of Underachievers, Normalachievers and Overachievers in Respect of Comprehensive Anxiety

Source	*DF*	*Sum of squares*	*Mean squares*	*F Ratio*	*Significance level*
Between groups	2	4266.8158	2133.4079		
Within groups	417	80334.1819	192.6479	11.0741	**
Total	419	84600.9976			

** Significant beyond the 0.01 level of probability

Table 4.13: Comparison of Mean Scores of Under, Normal and Overachievers in Respect of Comprehensive Anxiety

Mean	*Group*	*Group 3*	*Group 2*	*Group 1*
29.0000	Group 3			
31.4247	Group 2			
38.3667	Group 1	*	*	

* Denotes pairs of groups significantly different at the 0.050 level

The obtained F value 11.0741 was found to be significant beyond 0.01 level of probability, as it is more than the theoretical value of F. hence, it may be concluded that there is a significant difference between the scores of underachievers, normalachievers and overachievers in respect of comprehensive anxiety.

Further it was found that the mean scores of overachievers (29.0000) in respect of comprehensive anxiety is less than the mean scores of normalachievers (31.4247) and underachievers (38.3667). In this scale high scores indicate high anxiety and low scores indicate normal and low anxiety. The significant difference in the mean scores was found between underachievers and overachievers, and underachievers and normalachievers. There is no significant difference between normalachievers and overachievers. Hence, the first two sub hypotheses were rejected and the third sub hypothesis was accepted.

From this, it may be concluded that underachievers possess higher anxiety when compared to normalachievers and overachievers. Overachievers possess lower anxiety when compared to underachievers. From these findings it may be concluded that high anxiety is one of the causes of underachievement in Biology.

The results obtained in this study are confirmed by the findings reported by Bhaduri (1971) and Sushila Tandon (1977).

Hypothesis–6

There is no significant difference between underachievers, normalachievers and overachievers in respect of self-concept.

Sub Hypothesis

6.1. There is no significant difference in the mean scores of underachievers and normal achievers in respect of self-concept.

6.2. There is no significant difference in the mean scores of underachievers and overachievers in respect of self-concept.

6.3. There is no significant difference in the mean scores of normal achievers and overachievers in respect of self-concept.

The one way ANOVA details of the scores of underachievers, normalachievers and overachievers in respect of self-concept of first year P.U.C. Biology students of Chitradurga district are given in the following table.

Table 4.14: Summary of One way ANOVA of Underachievers, Normal Achievers and Overachievers in Respect of Self-concept

Source	*DF*	*Sum of squares*	*Mean squares*	*F Ratio*	*Significance level*
Between groups	2	11669.2072	5834.6036		
Within groups	417	92046.6404	220.7353	26.4326	**
Total	419	103715.8476			

** Significant beyond the 0.01 level of probability.

Since the 'F' value was found to be significant, the researcher was interested in knowing where exactly the difference lies. This was done using Duncan procedure. The value actually compared with Mean (J) – Mean (I) is –

$$10.5056 \times \text{Range} \times \sqrt{[1/N(I) + 1/N(J)]}$$

Table 4.15: Comparison of Mean Scores of Under, Normal and Overachievers in Respect of Self-concept

Mean	*Group*	*Group 1*	*Group 2*	*Group 3*
158.2444	Group 1			
167.4479	Group 2	*		
175.1690	Group 3	*	*	

* Denotes pairs of groups significantly different at the 0.050 level

The obtained F value 26.4326 was found to be significant beyond 0.01 level of probability, as it is more than theoretical value of F. Hence, it may be concluded that there is a significant difference between the scores of underachievers, normalachievers and overachievers in respect of self-concept.

Further it was found that the mean scores of overachievers (175.1690) in respect of self-concept is more than the mean scores of normalachievers (167.4479) and underachievers (158.2444). The significant difference in the mean scores was found between underachievers and normalachievers, underachievers and overachievers, and normalachievers and overachievers groups. Hence, all the three sub hypotheses were rejected. From this, it may be concluded that overachievers possess high self-concept when compared to underachievers and normalachievers, where as underachievers possess low self-concept when compared to normal and overachievers. The normal achievers have high self-concept when compared to underachievers. From these findings it may concluded that low self-concept is one of the causes of underachievement in Biology.

The results obtained in this study are corroborated by the results obtained in the studies that were conducted by Saxena (1972) and Shanta Kumari Agarwal (1976).

Hypothesis–7

There is no significant difference between underachievers, normalachievers and overachievers in respect of socio-economic status.

Sub Hypotheses

7.1. There is no significant difference in the mean scores of underachievers and normalachievers in respect of socio-economic status.

7.2. There is no significant difference in the mean scores of underachievers and overachievers in respect of socio-economic status.

7.3. There is no significant difference in the mean scores of normal achievers and overachievers in respect of socio-economic status.

The one way ANOVA details of the scores of underachievers, normalachievers and overachievers in respect of socio-economic status of first year P.U.C. Biology students of Chitradurga district are given in the following table.

Table 4.16: Summary of One Way ANOVA of Underachievers, Normalachievers and Overachievers in Respect of Socio-economic Status

Source	*DF*	*Sum of squares*	*Mean squares*	*F Ratio*	*Significance level*
Between groups	2	2525.0579	1262.5290		
Within groups	417	50928.5040	122.1307	10.3375	**
Total	419	53453.5619			

** Significant beyond the 0.01 level of probability

Since the 'F' value was found to be significant, the researcher was interested in knowing where exactly the difference lies. This was done using Duncan procedure. The value actually compared with Mean (J) – Mean (I) is –

$$7.8144 \times \text{Range} \times \sqrt{[1/N(I) + 1/N(J)]}$$

Table 4.17: Comparison of Mean Scores of Under, Normal and Overachievers in Respect of Socio-economic Status

Mean	*Group*	*Group 1*	*Group 2*	*Group 3*
29.3111	Group 1			
30.9459	Group 2			
36.8310	Group 3	*	*	

* Denotes pairs of groups significantly different at the 0.05 level

The obtained F value 10.3375 was found to be significant beyond 0.01 level of probability as it is more than the theoretical value of F. Hence, it may be concluded that there is a significant difference between the scores of underachievers, normalachievers and overachievers in respect of socio-economic status.

Further, it was found that the mean scores of overachievers (36.8310) in respect of socio-economic status is more than the mean scores of normalachievers (30.9459) and underachievers (29.3111). The significant difference in the mean scores was found between underachievers and overachievers, and normalachievers and overachievers group. There is no significant difference between the mean scores of underachievers and normalachievers. Hence, the first sub hypothesis was accepted and the other two sub hypotheses were rejected.

From this, it may be concluded that overachievers are from higher socio-economic status when compared to normalachievers and underachievers. Underachievers are from lower socio-economic status when compared to overachievers. From these findings it may be concluded that lower socio-economic status is one of the causes of underachievement in Biology.

The results obtained in this study are corroborated by the results obtained in the studies that were conducted by Srivastava (1967), Menon (1973), Shanta Kumari Agarwal (1976), Sharma (1978), and Puri, K (1987).

REFERENCES

1. Ferguson, George A. and Takane, Yoshio. *Statistical Analysis in Psychology and Education.* Sixth edition, Singapore: Mc Graw Hill Book Company, 1989, pp. 250-271.
2. Garett, Henry E. *Statistics in Psychology and Education.* Bombay: Vakils, Feffer and Simons Ltd., 1981, pp. 276-295.
3. Joseph, Alexander E. and Rajendran, K. "Influence of Self Concept, Sex, Area and Parents Education on Student's Adjustment Problems", *Journal of Education Research and Extension,* 28, 3, Jan 1992, pp. 129-137.
4. Mc. Guigan, F.J. *Experimental Psychology: A Methodological Approach* New Jersey: Prentice-Hall Inc., 1965, pp. 173-200.
5. Sarode, Vijayakumar, "A Study of Impact of Socio-Economic Status. Study Habits and Academic Motivation of Higher Secondary Students of the Rural Area". *The Progress of Education, LXXIII,* 6, Jan. 1999, pp. 122-124.

5

Summary of the Findings and Suggestions

In the previous chapter, the analysis and the interpretation of data have been presented in detail. In this chapter, the researcher presents a brief summary of the research which includes the statement of the problem, major objectives, hypotheses tested, methodology followed by the researcher, sampling and the tools and techniques used in the analysis of data. It also includes the conclusions drawn on the basis of interpretation of the findings, educational implications of the study and suggestions for further research.

Need and Importance of the Study

Wholesome development of the child is the primary concern of any established educational system. The academic development of the individual is the most important component of wholesome development. There are differences in the attainment of learning (academic) skills among individuals, moreover academic development is seldom homogeneous in the same individual. Further the most important issue in the academic development is often not in consonance with his ability and this brings us to the problem of underachievement which has been baffling researchers for several decades. Underachievement signifies that the child has not made the most of its abilities. It denotes that despite high potentialities, the child is lagging behind in academic achievement. This indeed is a great challenge which has to be met with great care because it involves serious loss to the individual leading to self under valuation, reflections of which are seen in unhappiness, frustration, revolt and withdrawal.

While discussing about the achievement of the students, the Education Commission (1964-66) observes that the problem of academic underachievement is of great concern to a developing country. Extraordinary talent unidentified, undeveloped and unexplored is a tremendous waste. The Commission has also mentioned the need for diagnosing the causes of low achievement which hinders the underachievers in coming upto the level of their full potential abilities and then to provide remedial treatment.

To a developing country like ours, this challenge is a of great social significance also as it involves colossal wastage of human potential. Therefore, it has to be encountered with profound care lest it should shake the very roots of nation's economic and social structure. Also one of the cardinal problems before educationists is to help each individual to achieve his optimum. Thus, the need for exploring scientifically the causal factors relating to underachievement is imperative.

As the investigator is interested in finding the causes of underachievement in Biology, it is worth to quote the words of Education commission (1964-66) about the importance of teaching Biology. In the words of Education commission. "The concept of Biology as a method of enquiry by means of accurate and confirmable observations, qualitatively and mathematically analysed and controlled experimentation should be impressed on the minds of young learners".

Biology is one of the core subjects taught at the pre-university science classes. It occupies an important place in the pre-university science curriculum because of its utilitarian, intellectual, aesthetic and social values. It is a matter of common experience of lecturers teaching Biology that, although many students have the capacity to learn well, their actual performance in Biology examinations is poor.

Many of the studies on underachievement in India and abroad have concentrated research mainly at the secondary level. The investigator feels that pre-university course is an important stage in the education of an individual. It is a stage to select diversified courses in his educational career. Most of the pre-university science students are aspiring for professional/technical/higher courses. In order to fulfil their desire, they will put maximum efforts in the academic work. In spite of this, many students will achieve less than their potential ability. In addition to this, Karnataka State Pre-university Board has introduced a new syllabus for the pre-university classes from the academic year 1995-96. The investigator decided to find out the causes of underachievement in Biology among the pre-university students, since the studies in this specific area are conspicuous by their absence.

Statement of the Problem

The problem of the present study is—"*An Investigation into the Factors Causing Underachievement in Biology among the First Year Pre-university Students of Chitradurga District*".

Objectives of the Study

The present study was undertaken with the following broad objectives:

1. To identify the underachievers in Biology among the first year pre-university students.
2. To identify the causes of underachievement in Biology among the first year pre-university students.
3. To suggest measures for the improvement of achievement of underachievers in Biology in the light of the identified causes of underachievement.

Specific Objectives of the Study

(*a*) To find out whether low attitude towards science is the causes of underachievement in Biology among the first year pre-university students.

(*b*) To find out whether low achievement motivation is the cause of underachievement in Biology among the first year pre-university students.

(*c*) To find out whether poor study habits is the cause of underachievement in Biology among the first year pre-university students.

(*d*) To find out whether poor adjustment is the cause of underachievement in Biology among the first year pre-university students.

(*e*) To find out whether higher comprehensive anxiety is the cause of underachievement in Biology among the first year pre-university students.

(*f*) To find out whether low self-concept is the cause of underachievement in Biology among the first year pre-university students.

(*g*) To find out whether low socio-economic status is the cause of underachievement in Biology among firs year pre-university students.

Hypotheses Tested

Based upon the discussion of variables and also keeping in view the objectives of the study, the following research hypotheses have been formulated.

1. There is no significant difference between underachievers, normalachievers and overachievers in respect of attitude towards science.

Sub hypotheses

1.1. There is no significant difference in the mean scores of underachievers and normalachievers in respect of attitude towards science.

1.2. There is no significant difference in the mean scores of underachievers and overachievers in respect of attitude towards science.

1.3. There is no significant difference in the mean scores of normalachievers and overachievers in respect of attitude towards science.

2. There is no significant difference between underachievers, normalachievers and overachievers in respect of achievement motivation.

Sub hypotheses

2.1. There is no significant difference in the mean scores of underachievers and normalachievers in respect of achievement motivation.

2.2. There is no significant difference in the mean scores of underachievers and overachievers in respect of achievement motivation.

2.3. There is no significant difference in the mean scores of normalachievers and overachievers in respect of achievement motivation.

3. There is no significant difference between underachievers, normalachievers and overachievers in respect of study habits.

Sub hypotheses

3.1. There is no significant difference in the mean scores of underachievers and normalachievers in respect of study habits.

3.2. There is no significant difference in the mean scores of underachievers and overachievers in respect of study habits.

3.3. There is no significant difference in the mean scores of normalachievers and overachievers in respect of study habits.

4. There is no significant difference between underachievers, normalachievers and overachievers in respect of adjustment.

Sub hypotheses

4.1. There is no significant difference in the mean scores of underachievers and normalachievers in respect of adjustment.

4.2. There is no significant difference in the mean scores of underachievers and overachievers in respect of adjustment.

4.3. There is no significant difference in the mean scores of normal achievers and overachievers in respect of adjustment.

5. There is no significant difference between underachievers, normalachievers and overachievers in respect of comprehensive anxiety.

Sub hypotheses

5.1. There is no significant difference in the mean scores of underachieves and normalachievers in respect of comprehensive anxiety.

5.2. There is no significant difference in the mean scores of underachievers and overachievers in respect of comprehensive anxiety.

5.3. There is no significant difference in the mean scores of normalachievers and overachievers in respect of comprehensive anxiety.

6. There is no significant difference between underachievers, normalachievers and overachievers in respect of self concept.

Sub hypotheses

6.1. There is no significant difference in the mean scores of underachievers and normalachievers in respect of self concept.

6.2. There is no significant difference in the mean scores of underachievers and overachievers in respect of self concept.

6.3. There is no significant difference in the mean scores of normalachievers and overachievers in respect of self concept.

7. There is no significant difference between underachievers, normalachievers and overachievers in respect of socio-economic status.

Sub hypotheses

7.1. There is no significant difference in the mean scores of underachievers and normalachievers in respect of socio-economic status.

7.2. There is no significant difference in the mean scores of underachievers and overachievers in respect of socio-economic status.

7.3. There is no significant difference in the mean scores of normalachievers and overachievers in respect of socio-economic status.

Methodology and Sampling

In the present study, the information was collected regarding the intelligence (predictor variable) and achievement in Biology to set a regression equation in order to identify underachievers, normalachievers and overachievers in Biology among the first year pre-university students.

The data regarding independent variables such as attitude towards science, achievement motivation, study habits, adjustment, comprehensive anxiety, self concept and socio-economic status of the first year pre-university students of Chitradurga district was collected to find out the causative effect of said factors on overachievers, normalachievers and underachievers in Biology.

The investigator has used the following tools for the collection of relevant data:

1. Group Test of Intelligence (Ahuja, 1976)—English version.

2. Achievement Test in Biology constructed by the researcher.

3. Science Attitude Scale of Avinash Grewal (1990).

4. Achievement Motive Test by Bhargava (1994).

5. Study Habits Inventory by Palsane and Sharma (1989).

6. Adjustment Inventory for College Students by Sinha and Singh (1980).

7. Comprehensive Anxiety Test by Sinha and Sinha (1990).

8. Self Concept Questionnaire by Rajkumar Saraswat (1992).

9. Kakkar's socio-economic Status Scale by Kakkar (1993).

Sampling

For the purpose of this study, 480 students were selected for the first year pre-university classes of Chatradurga district. Proportionate random sampling technique was used to select the sample. Totally ten pre-university colleges (with science combination) were selected proportionately on random basis, out of these 10 colleges; 4 were private urban colleges, 2 were private rural colleges, 2 were government urban colleges and 2 were government rural colleges. Proportion of rural and urban, government and private colleges is maintained in sampling. Urban and rural students are selected in the ratio of 2:1 (320:160) and boys and girls are also in the ratio of 2:1 (320:160).

Statistical Techniques Used for the Analysis of Data

The researcher has used the following statistical techniques for the analysis of data—co-efficient of correlation was calculated between dependent and independent variables, intercorrelations among independent variables.

The hypotheses formulated were tested using the single classification analysis of variance (one way ANOVA) and whenever 'F' value was found to be significant, Duncan procedure (Multiple range test) was used to test the significance of the mean difference of 2 groups.

Findings and Conclusions of the Study

The following are the findings of the present study:

1. Attitude of students towards science is positively and significantly related to achievement in Biology.
2. Achievement motivation is positively and significantly related to achievement in Biology.
3. There is positive and significant relationship between study habits and achievement in Biology.
4. There is negative and significant relationship between adjustment problems and achievement in Biology.
5. Anxiety is negatively and significantly related to achievement in Biology.
6. Self concept is positively and significantly related to achievement in Biology.
7. Socio-economic status is positively and significantly related to achievement in Biology.
8. Overachievers possess high attitude towards science when compared to normal achievers.
9. Overachievers possess high achievement motivation when compared to normalachievers and underachievers.
10. Underachievers have low achievement motivation when compared to normalachievers and overachievers.
11. Normalachievers have high achievement motivation when compared to underachievers and low achievement motivation than overachievers.

12. Overachievers possess good study habits when compared to underachievers.
13. Underachievers possess poor study habits when compared to normalachievers and overachievers.
14. Overachievers possess good adjustment when compared to underachievers and normal achievers.
15. Underachievers possess poor adjustment when compared to overachievers.
16. Overachievers possess lower anxiety when compared to underachievers.
17. Underachievers possess higher anxiety when compared to normalachievers and overachievers.
18. Overachievers possess high self concept when compared to underachievers and normalachievers.
19. Underachievers possess low self concept when compared to normalachievers and overachievers.
20. Normalachievers have high self concept when compared to underachievers and low self concept than overachievers.
21. Overachievers are from higher socio-economic status when compared to normalachievers and underachievers.
22. Underachievers are from lower socio-economic status when compared to overachievers.

Conclusions

The researcher has drawn the following conclusions on the basis of interpretation of the results which are as follows:

1. Low achievement motivation is the cause of underachievement in Biology.
2. Poor study habits is the cause of underachievement in Biology.

3. Poor adjustment is the cause of underachievement in Biology.
4. High comprehensive anxiety is the cause of underachievement in Biology.
5. Low self concept is the cause of underachievement in Biology.
6. Lower socio-economic status is the cause of underachievement in Biology among first year Pre-university science students of Chitradurga district.

Educational Implications of the Study

The following educational implications may be suggested based on the results obtained in this study.

1. Achievement motivation is significantly and positively related to achievement in Biology. Low achievement motivation is found to be the cause of underachievement in Biology where as high achievement leads to overachievement in Biology. Hence, there is a need for achievement motivation training for first year pre-university students to improve their achievement in Biology.

Prayag Mehta and P.C. Dandia (13:64-73), Mehta (14:46-47), and Markle A., Rinn, R.C. and Goodwin (11:567-574) have found that application of achievement motivation training programme helped underachievers to improve their academic performance.

2. The study reveals that there is a significant difference in the study habits of underachievers and overachievers, and underachievers and normalachievers. Poor study habits are found to be the cause of underachievement in Biology where as good study habits lead to overachievement in Biology. Pre-university colleges and teachers should provide opportunities or create such situations for the development of good study habits. Teachers should help

the learners in developing reading skills, note-taking, concentration, memorization, using dictionaries, group discussion and examination-taking skills.

Stasek, Edwin Daniel found that specialised educational conselling with selected groups of underachievers with regard to study habits helped them to bring their level of achievement into line with their potential. (18:2107)

Foreman, Forence, S. in his study of self reinforcement and study skill programmes with bright college underachievers found that study skill programmes helped a lot in improving academic achievement of pupils. (7:1430A)

Mary Suvarna found in her study that the experimental group of underachievers showed improvement in the study habits and scholastic achievement after the study skills programme. (12:210-215)

3. The study has brought to light that poor adjustment is the cause of underachievement in Biology, whereas good adjustment leads to overachievement in Biology. Pre-university colleges and teachers should bring in them the good home, health, social, emotional and educational adjustment, which will certainly help in improving their achievement in Biology. Teachers and parents should be given utmost care in dealing with the children positively so as to promote adjustment in these areas. A carefully organised programme of guidance and conselling should be made a available to all students especially for the poorly adjusted.

4. The study reveals that there is a significant difference in the comprehensive anxiety of underachievers and overachievers, underachiever and normalachievers. Overachievers possess lower anxiety when compared to underachievers; underachievers possess higher anxiety when compared to normal achievers and overachievers. Higher anxiety is found to be cause of underachievement in Biology. Anxiety is negatively and significantly related to achievement in Biology. In order

to overcome high anxiety among underachievers they should be given a feeling that they are secure, an atmosphere of friendliness, calmness, ease, sympathy, sociability, kindness and cooperativeness is to be created in the colleges and homes.

Sharma found that rational group counselling with anxious underachievers helped in reducing the anxiety of underachievers and resulted in the improvement of academic achievement. (17:132-137)

Tobias, S. and Weiss Broad, C. have found that the use of clearly articulated behaviour change models helped in reducing the anxiety of underachievers. (19:63-70)

5. The results of the study indicates that there is a significant difference in the self concept of underachievers, normalachievers and overachievers groups. Low self concept is found to be the cause of underachievement in Biology, whereas high self concept leads to overachievement in Biology. College and teachers should provide opportunities for the development of self concept in their learners. Every student must know about his capabilities and limitations in order to improve his achievement in Biology.

Dobbins in his study found that group counselling programmes helped in improving self concept and grade point averages of underachieving secondary school students. (4:428A)

6. This study has thrown adequate light on the effect of socio-economic status on the achievement in Biology. SES is positively and significantly related to achievement in Biology. Low SES is found to be the cause of underachievement in Biology, whereas high SES leads to overachievement in Biology. Major components of SES, as such lie outside the preview of educational practitioners who have little control over them. However education can create such conditions

in the school as well, leading to better performance of the children. Compensatory education programmes may be scientifically planned and imparted to such categories of children who are socially and economically backward. Educational institutions should keep a comprehensive chart relating to the family background of each child along with his progress chart. This may help to find out the backwardness relating to family and may provide suitable measures for minimizing the grave effect of the incidence of underachievement.

7. Guidance and counselling treatments with respect to underachievers which include case conferences, individual counselling, small group counselling, group counselling programmes, quiz programmes and group discussions. Calhoun (2:1397-1398), Winborn (20:550-551), Edward Terry Irvine (5:2421), Brusnahan (1:3273-A), Dandapani (3:452), Fernandes (6:531), Kohli and Devinder (10:30-36) and Dobbins (4:428-A) found that such counselling sessions stimulate interest among underachievers, arouse desire for emulation, raise their level of aspiration and show consistent improvement in their achievement.

8. Teachers and learners must have clear understanding of objectives of teaching Biology at the pre-university level. At present the emphasis is on knowledge objective and due weightage was not given to understanding, application and skill. The model question paper pattern suggested by the Pre-university Board of Karnataka in their syllabus book clearly indicates that more than 40 per cent weightage is given to knowledge objective (8:125-154). Hence, there is a need to rectify the present pattern and give more weightages for understanding, application and skill objectives.

The researcher found that majority of the students did not do well in the drawing part of the achievement test in Biology. It clearly indicates that emphasis was not given on the development of drawing skills in the learners. Biology is a subject where there is a lot of scope for the development of psychomotor objectives (skills) in its learners. Biology lecturers at the P.U.C. classes must give priority for the development of required objectives in their learners.

John and Abraham have found that the development of clear understanding of objectives of a subject help in improving the level of achievement of underachievers among college students. (9:454)

9. Most of the students at the pre-university classes with Physics. Chemistry, Mathematics and Biology combination entered the course with positive attitude towards the science. They are in need of proper help and guidance from the concerned teachers to move in the right direction. Teachers must use diagnostic tests of diagnose the causes for the backwardness in learning and take up remedial teaching which will certainly help in overcoming underachievement in Biology at the pre-university classes.

It is hoped that the study has revealed some useful information regarding the nature of causal variable of underachievement in Biology of first year pre-university students of Chitradurga district. It is the fervent belief of the investigator that the findings of the study would be of some help to understand the grave problem arising from the incidence of underachievement and to devise adequate educational practices helpful for minimizing it.

Limitations of the Study

1. The sample included the students of the first year pre-university science (with PCMB combination) classes only.
2. Sample covers the randomly selected rural and urban pre-university colleges of Chitradurga district.
3. Though a number of factors are related to underachievement, only relationship of factors such as

attitude towards science, achievement motivation, study habits, adjustment, comprehensive anxiety, self concept and socio-economic status were studied.

Suggestions for Further Research

1. Comprehensive studies on similar lines may be taken up with more social and personality variables.
2. Similar studies can be conducted in different curricular science subjects such as Physics, Chemistry and Mathematics at the pre-university level.
3. Similar studies can be conducted in different curricular subjects at the different levels such as primary, secondary and college.
4. Follow up study is advisable to find out the persistence of underachievement in Biology at different levels of education.
5. Studies may also be conducted to find out the nature of underachievement in different subjects. This may help to find out whether there is any relation between aptitude and underachievement. It may also help to verify whether a learner who is an underachiever in one subject is uniformly underachieving in other subjects and if so, what are the common personality and social variables related to underachievement in general.
6. Different types of statistical techniques such as factorial analysis for a wide variety of variables, correlation methods and 't' test may also be attempted for finding out the incidence of underachievement.
7. In the light of the findings of the present study, a programme may be evolved and tried on a small group of underachievers to see how far they are useful in improving the achievement in Biological science among first year pre-university students in the local of the study.

REFERENCES

1. Brusnahan, Brother Joseph. "A Study of the Effect of Small Group Counselling on 9th Grade Underachievers". The University of Tennessee, 1996. *Dissertation Abstracts International,* 30, 8, Feb. 1970, p. 3273-A.

2. Calhoun, Semuel Reed. "The Effect of Counselling on a Group of Eighth Grade Underachievers". University of Pittsburgh, 1956. *Dissertation Abstracts,* 16, 8, Aug. 1956. pp. 1397-1398.

3. Dandapani, S. "A Study of the Effect of a Group Guidance Programme upon the Academic Achievement of High School Underachievement". Mysore University, 1976. In Buch, M.B. (Ed.), *Third Survey of Research in Education (1978-1983)* New Delhi: N.C.E.R.T., 1986.

4. Dobbins, Dolores Pauline Farries. "Effects of a Group Counselling Programme on Grade Point Average and Non Cognitive Factors of Self Concept among Underachieving Secondary School Students". Auburn University, 1989. *Dissertation Abstracts International,* 52, 7, Aug. 1991, p. 428-A.

5. Edward, Terry Irvine. "Increased Individual Counselling as a Factor in Improving Subject Matter Grades of Underachieving Superior High School Students". University of Southern California, 1962. *Dissertation Abstracts,* 23, 7, Jan 1963. p. 2421.

6. Fernandes, L. "A Study of the Effect of Guidance and Counselling on the Academic Achievement of Underachieving Pre-Adolescent and Adolescent Girls". Mysore University, 1984. In Buch, M.B. (Ed.), *Fourth Survey of Research in Education (1983-1988),* Vol. 1, New Delhi: N.C.E.R.T., 1991.

7. Foreman, Forence S. "Study of Self Reinforcement and Study Skills Programmes with Bright College Underachievers". The University of Nabraska, 1969. *Dissertation Abstracts International,* 30, 4, Oct. 1969, p. 1430-A.

8. Government of Karnataka. *Regulations, Courses of Study, Scheme of Examination and Syllabus for 2 year Pre-University Course, part-III (Science and Mathematics).* Bangalore: Department of Pre-university Education, 1995, Director, Department of Printing Stationary and Publications, Bangalore, pp. 125-154.

9. John P., and Abraham M. "A Study of Underachievement among College Students with a view to Formulating a Guidance

Profile". UGC Financed, Kerala University, 1981. In Buch, M.B. (Ed.), *Third Survey of Research in Education (1979-1983).* New Delhi: N.C.E.R.T., 1986.

10. Kohli and Devinder. "Effect of Individual Counselling on Bright Underachievers". *Asian Journal of Psychology and Education,* 17, 3, July 1986, pp. 30-86.

11. Markle, A., Rinn, R.C. and Goodwin. "Effect of Achievement Motivation Training on Academic Performance of Underachievers". *Psychological Reports,* 42, 2, October 1980, pp. 567-574.

12. Mary Survarna. *The Effectiveness of Training in Study Skills for High School Underachievers in Relation to their Scholastic Achievement.* Unpublished Doctoral Dissertation, Kuvempu University, 1997, pp. 210-215.

13. Mehta, Prayag and Dandia P.C. "Motivation Training for Educational Development—A Follow-up Study of Bright Underachievers". *Indian Educational Review.* 5, 2, July 1970, pp. 64-73.

14. Mehta, Prayag. "Achievement Motivation Training for Educational Development". *Indian Educational Review,* 3, 1, 1968, pp. 46-47.

15. Nagappa, P. Shahpur. "Study Habits of Secondary School Students of Mysore City". *Experiments in Education,* XXII, 9, Sept. 1995.

16. Nava, Butler-Por. "The Phenomenon and Treatment of Academic Underachievement in Children of Superior and Average Ability". University of Wales (UK) 1982. *Dissertation Abstracts International,* 49, 9, March 1989.

17. Sharma, K.L. "Rational Group Counselling with Anxious Underachievers". *Canadian Counseller.* 9, 2, April 1975, pp. 132-137.

18. Stasek, Erwin Daniel. "The Effects of Specialised Educational Counselling with Selected Groups of Underachievers at the Secondary School Level". Northwestern University, 1955. *Dissertation Abstracts,* 15, 11, Nov. 1955, p. 2107.

19. Tobias, S. and Weissbrod, C. "Anxiety and Mathematics—An Update". *Harvard Educational Review,* 50, 1, Feb. 1980, pp. 63-70.

20. Winborn, Bob Burton. "The Effectiveness of Short Term Group Counselling upon the Academic Achievement of Potentially Superior but Underachieving College Freshman". Indiana University 1960. *Dissertation Abstracts,* 21, 3, Sept. 1960, pp. 550-551.

Bibliography

1. Abraham, M, *Factors Relating to Underachievement in English.*Trivandrum: Department of Publications, University of Kerala, 1978.

2. Agarwal, S. "The Study of Causes and their Remedial Measures of Two Groups of X and XII Class of Relatively Identical Intelligence but Differing in Educational Achievements". Gorakhpur University, 1982. In Buch M.B. (Ed.), *Fourth Survey of Research in Education (1983-1988).* Vol. 1, New Delhi: National Council of Educational Research and Training, 1991.

3. Agrawal, Shanta Kumari, "A Psycho-social Study of Academic Underachievement". University of Rajasthan, 1976. *Indian Dissertation Abstracts,* 10, 3 and 4, July-Dec. 1981, pp. 311-316.

4. Ahuja, G.C. *Mannual for Group Test of Intelligence.* Agra: National Psychological Corporation, 1976, pp. 1-36.

5. Anastasi, Anne. *Psychological Testing.* Third edition. London: The Mac Millan Company, Collier—Mac Millan Limited, 1968.

6. Anderson. J., Durston, H.B. and Poole. M. *Thesis and Assignment Writing,* New Delhi: Wiley Eastern Limited, 1970.

7. Armstrong, Marion Elizabeth. "A Comparison of the Interests and Social Adjustment of Underachievers and Normalachievers at the Secondary Level". The University of Connecticut, 1955. *Dissertation Abstracts International,* 15, 8, Aug. 1955, pp. 1349-1350.

8. Barret, H.G. "An Intensive Study of 32 Gifted Children". *Personnel and Guidance Journal,* 36, 1957, pp. 192-194.

9. Base. *CET—Correspondence Course, Biology.* Vol. 1 to 10, Bangalore: No. 14, Bull Temple Road, Basavanagudi, 1994.

10. Beedawat, Sher Singh. "A Study of Academic Underachievement Among Students". University of Rajasthan, 1976, *Indian Dissertation Abstracts,* 12, 14, Jan.-Dec. 1984, p. 188.

11. Bently, Tom. *Learning Beyond the Classroom.* London: Routledge, 1988, pp. 73-98.

12. Best, J.W. and Kahn, J.V. *Research in Education.* Fifth edition. New Delhi: Prentice-Hall of India Pvt. Ltd., 1986.

13. Bhaduri, A. "Comparative Study of Certain Psychological Characteristics of the Over and the Underachievers in Higher Secondary Schools". Calcutta University, 1971. In Buch, M.B. (Ed.), *Second Survey of Research in Education (1972-78)* Baroda: Society for Educational Research and Development, 1979.

14. Bhargava, V.P. *Revised Manual for Achievemnt Motive Test.* Agra: National Psychological Corporation, 1994, pp. 2-7.

15. Bricklin, P. and Bricklin, P.M. *Bright Poor Grades: The Psychology of Underachievement.* New York: Delacorte Press. 1966.

16. Brusnahan, Brother Joseph. "A Study of the Effect of Small Group Counselling on 9th Grade Underachievers". The University of Tennessee, 1996. *Dissertation Abstracts International,* 30, 8, Feb. 1970, p. 3273-A.

17. Calhoun, Semuel Reed. "The Effect of Counselling on a Group of Eighth Grade Underachievers". University of Pittsburgh, 1956. *Dissertation Abstracts,* 16, 8, Aug. 1956. pp. 1397-1398.

18. Cattel, R.B., Sealey, A.P. and Sevency, A.B. "What can Personality and Motivation Service Traits Measurement Add to the Prediction of School Achievement?" *British Journal of Educational Psychology,* 36, 1966, pp. 280-296.

19. Chaudhari, V.P. Jain. "Factors Contributing to Academic Underachievement". Nagpur University, 1975. In Buch, M.B. (Ed.), *Third Survey of Research in Education (1978-1983).* New Delhi: N.C.E.R.T., 1986.

20. Chauhan, S.S. *Advanced Educational Pscyhology.* Fourth revised edition, New Delhi: Vikas Publishing House Pvt. Ltd., 1962.

21. Cronbach, Lee. J. *Essentials of Psychological Testing.* Third Education, Harper and Row Publishers Inc., 1970.

22. Dandapani, S. "A Study of the Effect of a Group Guidance Programme upon the Academic Achievement of High School Underachievement". Mysore University, 1976. In Buch, M.B. (Ed.), *Third Survey of Research in Education (1978-1983)* New Delhi: N.C.E.R.T., 1986.

23. Deo, Prathibha. "Underachievers: A Challenge to Educators". *NIE Journal,* 2, 4, March 1968, pp. 5-13.

24. Deo, Prathibha., and Gupta, Arun Kumar. "A Comparison of the Criteria for Identifying Over and Underachievers". *Indian Educational Review,* 7, 1, Jan. 1972, pp. 153-167.

25. Deshpande, A.S. "A Study of Determinants of Achievement of Students at the SSC Examination in the Pune Division of Maharashtra State". Poona University, 1984. In Buch M.B. (Ed.), *Fourth Survey of Research in Education (1983-1988),* Vol. 1, New Delhi: National Council of Educational Research and Training, 1991.

26. Dhaliwal, A.S. and Saini, B.S. "A Study of the Prevalence of Academic Underachievement Among High School Students". *Educational Review,* 10, 1, Jan. 1975, pp. 90-107.

27. Dobbins, Dolores Pauline Farries. "Effects of a Group Counselling Programme on Grade Point Average and Non Cognitive Factors of Self Concept among Underachieving Secondary School Students". Auburn University, 1989. *Dissertation Abstracts International,* 52, 7, Aug. 1991, p. 428-A.

28. Dowd, R.J. Underachieving Students of High Capacity. *Journal of Higher Education,* 22, 1962, pp. 327-330.

29. Dubois, Philip H. *An Introduction of Psychological Statistics.* New York: Harper and Row, 1965.

30. Ebel, Robert L. *Measuring Educational Achievement.* Prentice-Hall, India.

31. Ebel, Robert L. and Frisbie, David A. *Essentials of Educational Measurement.* Fifth edition, New Delhi: Prentice Hall of India Private Limited, 1991, pp. 231-232.

32. Edward, Terry Irvine. "Increased Individual Counselling as a Factor in Improving Subjects Matter Grades of Underachieving Superior High School Students". University of Southern California, 1962. *Dissertation Abstracts,* 23, 7, Jan 1963. p. 2421.

33. Farquhar, W.W. and Payne, D.A. "A Classification and Comparison of Techniques used in Selecting Under and Overachievers". *Personnel and Guidance Journal,* 1964, 42, pp. 674-684.

34. Ferguson, G.A. *Statistical Analysis in Psychology and Education.* Fourth edition, Tokyo: Mc. Graw Hill, Kogakusha Ltd., 1976.

35. Ferguson, George A. and Takane, Yoshio. *Statistical Analysis in Psychology and Education.* Sixth edition, Singapore: Mc Graw Hill Book Company, 1989, pp. 250-271.

36. Fernandes, L. "A Study of the Effect of Guidance and Counselling on the Academic Achievement of Underachieving Pre-Adolescent and Adolescent Girls". Mysore University, 1984. In Buch, M.B. (Ed.), *Fourth Survey of Research in Education (1983-1988),* Vol. 1, New Delhi: National Council of Educational Research and Training, 1991.'

37. Fine, Benjamin. *Underachievers: How They can be Helped.* New York: E.P. Dutton and Co., Inc., 1967.

38. Foreman, Forence S. "Study of Self Reinforcement and Study Skills Programmes with Bright College Underachievers". The University of Nabraska, 1969. *Dissertation Abstracts International,* 30, 4, Oct. 1969, p. 1430-A.

39. Frankel, E. "A Comparative Study of Achieving and Underachieving High School Boys of High Intellectual Ability". *Journal of Educational Research,* 53, Jan. 1960, pp. 172-180.

40. Garret, Henry E. *Statistics in Psychology and Education.* Bombay: Vikils, Feffer and Simons Ltd., 1981. pp. 151-181, 365.

41. Ghuman, M.S. "A Study of Aptitudes, Personality Traits and Achievement Motivation of Academic Overachievers and Underachievers". Rohtak University, 1976. In Buch, M.B. (Ed.), *Third Survey of Research in Education (1978-1983),* New Delhi: National Council of Educational Research and Training, 1986.

42. Goldaman, L. *Using Test in Counselling,* New York: Appleton—Century Crofts, 1961.

43. Government of India. *Report of the Education Commission (1964-66).* Education and National Development, New Delhi: Ministry of Education, 1966.

44. Government of Karnataka. *Regulations, Courses of Study, Scheme of Examination and Syllabus for 2 year Pre-University Course, part-III (Science and Mathematics).* Bangalore: Department of Pre-university Education, 1995, Director,

Department of Printing Stationary and Publications, Bangalore, pp. 125-154.

45. Government of Karnataka. *Statistics of the Second Year Pre-University Result (1992-1996).* Bangalore: Karnataka State Pre-University Board, 1996.

46. Gowan, J.C. "Underachievement Revisited". *High School Journal,* 48, 1964, pp. 117-119.

47. Gowan, J.C. "Dynamics of Underachievement of Gifted Students" *Indian Educational Review,* National Council of Educational Research and Training, 3, 2, July 1968, pp. 153-167.

48. Grewal, Avinash. *Manual for Science Attitude Scale.* Agra: National Psychological Corporation, 1990, pp. 2-8.

49. Gronlund, Norman E. *Measurement and Evaluation in Teaching.* Third edition, New York: Mac Millan Publishing Co., Inc., 1976, p. 285.

50. Guilford, J.P. *Psychometric Methods.* Second edition. New Delhi: Tata McGraw Hill Publishing Co. Ltd., 1984, pp. 414-464.

51. Guilford, J.P. *Fundamental Statistics in Psychology and Education.* Fourth edition. New York: McGraw Hill Company, 1965.

52. Harper, Edwin A. Jr. and Harper, Erika S. *Preparing Objective Examinations, A Handbook for Teachers, Students and Examiners.* New Delhi: Prentice Hall of India Private Limited, 1992.

53 Hivighurst, R.J. Stevena, E. and Dehaan, H.F. "A Survey of Education of the Gifted Children". Chicago: *Supplementary Educational Monograph,* No. 33, Univ. of Chicago Press, 1955.

54. Hocking, Thomas Kenneth. "A Case Study Approach to the Understanding of Underachieving Students in a Selected High School Setting". The University of Wisconsin, 1965, *Dissertation Abstracts International,* 26, 9, March 1966, p. 5235.

55. *Institute for Scientific Information,* Current Contents—Social and Behavioural Sciences (1995-1999), ISI, 3501, Market Street, Philadelphia, USA.

56. Iyer. K.K. "Some Factors Related to Underachievement in Mathematics of Secondary School Students". 1977. In Buch,

M.B. (Ed.), *Third Survey of Research in Education,* New Delhi: National Council of Educational Research and Training, 1987.

57. Jahan. Q. "A Study of Personality Profiles of Students of Science, Arts and Commerce at the Higher Secondary Level of Education in Relation to their Academic Achievement". Aligarh Muslim University, 1985. In Buch, M.B. (Ed.), *Fourth Survey of Research in Education (1983-1988)* Vol. 1. New Delhi: National Council of Educational Research and Training, 1991.

58. John, C.D. "*Predictive Correlates of Creativity of IX Standard Students in the City of Bangalore*". Unpublished Doctoral Dissertation, Bangalore University, Bangalore: 1996, pp. 119-122.

59. John P., and Abraham M. "A Study of Underachievement among College Students with a view to Formulating a Guidance Profile". UGC Financed, Kerala University, 1981. In Buch, M.B. (Ed.), *Third Survey of Research in Education (1979-1983).* New Delhi: National Council of Educational Research and Training, 1986.

60. Joseph, Alexander E. and Rajendran, K. "Influence of Self Concept, Sex, Area and Parents Education on Student's Adjustment Problems". *Journal of Education Research and Extension,* 28, 3, Jan. 1992, pp. 129-137.

61. Kakkar, S.B. *Manual for Kakkar Socio-Economic Status Scale.* Agra: National Psychological Corporation, 1993, pp. 3-11.

62. Kerlinger, Fred. N. *Foundations of Behavioural Research.* Second edition, Delhi: Surjeet Publications, 1983.

63. Kohli and Devinder. "Effect of Individual Counselling on Bright Underachievers". *Asian Journal of Psychology and Education,* 17, 3, July 1986, pp. 30-86.

64. Kowitz, G.T. and Armstrong, C.M. "Patterns of Academic Development". *Journal of Educational Development,* 2, 1965, pp. 207-211.

65. Kuppuswamy B. *A Text Book of Child Behaviour and Development.* Second revised edition, New Delhi: Vikas Publishing House Pvt. Ltd., 1980.

66. Lisa, Friedenberg. *Psychological Testing—Design, Analysis and Use.* Massachusetts: Allyn and Bacon, A Simon and Schuster Company, Needham Heights, 1955, pp. 480-490.

67. Maitra. Krishna. *Gifted Underachievers: A Challenge in Education.* New Delhi: Discovery Publishing House, 1991.

68. Mathew, Thomas. "Some Personality Factors Related to Underachievement in Science". University of Kerala, 1976. *Indian Dissertation Abstract,* Jan. –March 1979, pp. 77-80.

69. Matsunaga, Allen Sadao. "A Comparative Study of Ninth Grade Male Underachievers and Achievers on Selected Factors related to Achievement". University of Illinois 1971. *Dissertation Abstracts International,* 32, 10, April 1972, p. 5614-A.

70. Markle, A., Rinn, R.C. and Goodwin. "Effect of Achievement Motivation Training on Academic Performance of Underachievers". *Psychological Reports,* 42, 2, October 1980, pp. 567-574.

71. Mary Survarna. *The Effectiveness of Training in Study Skills for High School Underachievers in Relation to their Scholastic Achievement.* Unpublished Doctoral Dissertation, Kuvempu University, 1997, pp. 210-215.

72. M.C.C. Publications, *Biology.* Common Entrance Test 1995, Bangalore: No. 3, 16th Cross, 3rd Block, Jayanagar, 1995.

73. Mc. Guigan, F.J. *Experimental Psychology: A Methodological Approach.* New Jersey: Prentice-Hall Inc., 1965, pp. 173-178, 188-200.

74. Mehta, C.P. "An Investigation into the Effect of Some Psychological Factors in School Achievement of SC and ST Students and the States as Identified by the Baxi Commission in Saurastra". Ph.D., Edu., SPU, 1987. In Buch M.B. (Ed.), *Fourth Survey of Research in Education (1983-1988),* Vol. 1, New Delhi: National Council of Educational Research and Training, 1991.

75. Mehta, Prayag and Dandia P.C. "Motivation Training for Educational Development—A Follow-up Study of Bright Underachievers". *Indian Educational Review.* 5, 2, July 1970, pp. 64-73.

76. Mehta, Prayag. "Achievement Motivation Training for Educational Development". *Indian Educational Review,* 3, 1, 1968, pp. 46-47.

77. Menon, S.K. "A Comparative Study of the Personality Characteristics of Overachievers and Underachievers of High

Ability". Kerala University, 1973. In Buch, M.B. (Ed.), *Second Survey of Research in Education,(1972-78)* Baroda: Society for Educational Research and Development, 1979.

78. Miller, Arlyn Hochberg. "A Study of Personality Differences of Achieving and Underachieving Eleventh Grade Students". Temple University, 1965. *Dissertation Abstracts International,* 26, 8, Feb. 1966, p. 4454.

79. Mohanty, Susandhya. *Teaching of Science in Secondary Schools.* New Delhi: Deep and Deep Publication, F-159, Rajouri Garden, 1996, pp. 82-101.

80. Nagappa, P. Shahpur. "Study Habits of Secondary School Students of Mysore City". *Experiments in Education,* XXII, 9, Sept. 1995.

81. Nair, Jagannadan, *Identification of Some Personality Variables which Discriminate between High Intelligence Normal Achievers and High Intelligence Underachievers in Maths.* Unpublished M.Ed., Dissertation, University of Kerala, 1974.

82. Nair, P.K.G. et al., *A Text Book of Biology.* Vol. 1. (First year Pre-university), Bombay: Himalaya Publishing House, 1995.

83. Nair, Sankaran C.K. *"Factors Related to Underachievement in Biology of Secondary School Students".* Unpublished Doctoral Dissertation, University of Calicut, 1987.

84. National Council of Education Research and Training. *National Policy on Education—1986.* Resource Material. New Delhi: National Council of Educational Research and Training, 1987.

85. Nava, Butler-Por. "The Phenomenon and Treatment of Academic Underachievement in Children of Superior and Average Ability". University of Wales (UK) 1982. *Dissertation Abstracts International,* 49, 9, March 1989.

86. Pal, S.K., and Saxena P.C. "The Problems of Over, Under and Normalachieving College Students". Department of Education, Allahabad University, 1970. (N.C.E.R.T. financed) In Buch, M.B. (Ed.), *A Survey of Research in Education.* Baroda: Centre of Advanced Studies in Education, 1974.

87. Palsane, M.N. and Sadhna Sharma, *Manual for Palsane and Sharma Study Habit Inventory.* Agra: National Psychological Corporation, 1990, pp. 1-8.

88. Puri, K. "Personality Traits and Self Concept of 16-18 years old Underachievers". Avadh University, 1987. In Buch, M.B.

(Ed.), *Fourth Survey of Research in Education (1983-88)*. Vol. 1, New Delhi: National Council of Educational Research and Training, 1991.

89. Rathaiah, L,. and Bhaskara Rao, D. *Achievement Correlates.* New Delhi: Discovery Publishing House, 1997, pp. 53-59.

90. Saraswat, Rajkumar, *Mannual for Self Concept Questionnaire.* Agra: National Psychological Corporation, 1984, pp. 3-7.

91. Sarin, C. *Objectives Evaluation in Biology*. New Delhi: Tata McGraw Hill Publishing Company Ltd., 1989.

92. Sarode, Vijayakumar. "A Study of Impact of Socio-Economic Status, Study Habits and Academic Motivation of Higher Secondary Students of the Rural Area", *The Progress of Education,* LXXIII, 6, Jan. 1999, pp. 122-124.

93. Sarojamma, Y.H. *A Comparative Study of Reading Ability and Social Maturity of Over, Normal and Underachievers of VII Standard.* Unpublished Doctoral Dissertation, Bangalore University, Bangalore, 1989.

94. Saxena, P.C. "A Study of Interests, Need Patterns and Adjustment Problems of Over and Underachievers". Allahabad University, 1972. *Indian Dissertation Abstracts.* 17, July-Sept. 1988, pp. 258-265.

95. Seetharam, P.L. Thulajappa, Y. and Chavan, R.R. *Text Book of Biology.* Vol. 1. Bangalore: Expert Educational Publishers, 1996.

96. Seetharam, P.L. Thulajappa, Y. *A Text Book of Biology.* (First year Pre-university). Bangalore: Expert Educational Enterprises, 1995.

97. Shahapur, N.P. *An Investigation into the Causes of Underachievement in Secondary School Mathematics".* Unpublished Doctoral Dissertation, Karnataka University, Dharwad, 1994.

98. Sharma, G.S. "Attributes of Underachieving Undergraduate Students". Meerut University, 1978. In Buch, M.B. (Ed.), *Second Survey of Research in Education.* Baroda: Society for Educational Research and Development, 1979.

99. Sharma, K.L. "Rational Group Counselling with Anxious Underachievers". *Canadian Counseller.* 9, 2, April 1975, pp. 132-137.

100. Shaw, M.C. and Mc. Cuen. "The Aspect of Academic Underachievement of Bright Children". *Journal of Educational Psychology,* 51, 1960, pp. 103-108.

101. Sinha, A.K.P. and Singh, R.P. *Manual for Adjustment Inventory for College Stduents.* Agra: National Psychological Corporation, 1980, pp. 2-8.

102. Sinha, A.K.P. and Sinha, L.K.P. *Manual for Sinha's Comprehensive Anxiety Test.* Agra: National Psychological Corporation, 1990, pp. 3-7.

103. Skinner, Charles, E. *Educaitonal Psychology,* Fourth edition, New Delhi: Prentice-Hall of India Pvt. Ltd., 1984.

104. Snellgrove, John Louis. "A Study of Relationships between Certain Personal and Socio-Economic Factors and Underachievement". University of Albana, 1960. *Dissertation Abstracts International,* 21, 7, Jan. 1961, p. 1859.

105. Spiering, M.F. *A Study of Past Achievement Patterns of Achievement and Underachieving Eighth Grade Students.* Published Doctoral Dissertation, University of Fordham, 1963. In Nair, Shankaran C.K., Factors Related to Underachievement in Biology of Secondary School Students. Unpublished Doctoral Dissertation, University of Calicut, 1987.

106. Srivastava, A.K. "An Investigation into the Factors Related to Educational Underachievement". Patna University, 1967. In Buch, M.B. (Ed.), *A Survey of Research in Education,* Baroda: Centre of Advanced Studies in Education, 1974.

107. Stasek, Erwin Daniel. "The Effects of Specialised Educational Counselling with Selected Groups of Underachievers at the Secondary School Level". Northwestern University, 1955. *Dissertation Abstracts,* 15, 11, Nov. 1955, p. 2107.

108. Stoner, William Gerald. "Factors Related to the Underachievement of High School Students". Stanford University, 1956. *Dissertation Abstracts International,* 17, 1, Jan. 1957, pp. 96-97.

109. Tandon, Sushila, "A Psychological and Ecological Study of Underachievers". Banaras Hindu University, 1977. *Indian Dissertation Abstracts,* Jan.-Dec. 1985, pp. 216-220.

110. Terry, Patricia Ann Simpson. "A Study of Self-esteem in Underachieving Students is a Population of At-Risk Secondary

Students". The University of Mississippi, 1994. *Dissertation Abstracts International,* 55, 7, Jan. 1995, p. 1899-A.

111. Thorndike, R. *Personal Selection Test and Measurement Techniques.* New York: John Wiley and Sons Inc., February 1966, p. 245.

112. Tobias, S. and Weissbrod, C. "Anxiety and Mathematics—An Update". *Harvard Educational Review,* 50, 1, Feb. 1980, pp. 63-70.

113. Tolor, Alexander. "Incidence of Underachievement at the High School Level". *The Journal of Educational Research,* National Council of Educational Research and Training 63, 2, Oct. 1969, pp. 63-64.

114. Tuckman, Bruce, W. *Conducting Educational Research.* New York: Harcourt Brace Jovanovich Inc., 1978, pp. 58-59.

115. Vashistha, K.K. "A Comparative Study of the Adjustment of High and Low Achieving Indian Pupils at Higher Secondary Level". *Journal of Educational Research and Extension,* 27, 3, Jan. 1991, pp. 181-191.

116. Wageman. "Persistence of Ability—Achievement Discrepancies and Kuder Scores". *Personnel and Guidance Journal,* 43, 1964, pp. 383-389.

117. Wellington, C.B., and Wellington, J. *The Underachievers: Challenges and Guidelines.* Chicago: Rand Mc. Nally Curriculum Series, Rand Mc Nally and Company, 1964, p. 1.

118. Winborn, Bob Burton. "The Effectiveness of Short Term Group Counselling upon the Academic Achievement of Potentially Superior but Underachieving College Freshman". Indian University 1960. *Dissertation Abstracts,* 21, 3, Sept. 1960, pp. 550-551.

119. Yaworski, Jo Ann, "Why Students Succeed or Fail: Theories of Underachieving Affluent College Students". State University of New York at Albany, 1996. *Dissertation Abstracts International,* 57, 4, Oct. 1996, p. 1543-A.

120. Yu, Shirely Lynn, "Cognitive Strategy use and Motivation in Underachieving Students". The University of Michigan, 1996. *Dissertation Abstracts International,* 57, 11, May 1997, p. 4652-A.

Index